sweet zen

Also on the teaching of Cheri Huber

sweet zen

dharma talks from cheri huber

edited by sara jenkins

present perfect books

Publisher's Cataloging-in-Publication
(Provided by Quality Books, Inc.)

Huber, Cheri.
    Sweet Zen : dharma talks from Cheri Huber /
edited by Sara Jenkins. — 1st ed.
    p. cm
    LCCN: 00-130514
    ISBN: 0-9630784-4-5

    1. Zen Buddhism. 2. Spiritual life--Zen
Buddhism. 3. Man (Buddhism)   I. Jenkins, Sara.
II. Title.

BQ9265.H83 2000   294.3'927
                    QBI00-500141

Cover and design by The Design Den, Denver/Pocatello

The quotation on the opposite page is used with permission from
The Shambhala Sun magazine.

Present Prefect Books
P.O. Box 1212, Lake Junaluska, NC 28745

The experience of studying [the dharma] is so sweet,
it is like honey.

You cannot get enough of it. It is addictive.

It is like going to a wonderful symphony,
and every sound is perfect.

There is a sense that you are being effortlessly led along.

The composer, the music, the people
playing each instrument—all are in complete unity.

There is that kind of unity in the dharma.

Each word of the dharma is a bodhisattva
who is communicating to you.

Sakyong Mipham Rinpoche
Shambhala Sun, March 2000

❀ contents ❀

❧ preface: the opposite of tough ❧

Years ago, I left one of my first long Zen retreats with a vision of myself as *tough*. The retreat involved not only a rigorous schedule of sitting in meditation for many hours a day but also various forms of renunciation: silence, not looking at others, not reading or writing, a spartan diet, and no caffeine.

In the valley below the retreat center, I stopped to get gas at a full-service general store, where my new self-image met its first challenge. Would a truly tough person succumb to the urge to buy an iced tea? I asked myself. No, I answered firmly. Not that I would never again enjoy iced tea, but succumbing at the very first opportunity would be the opposite of tough.

At the check-out counter, I found myself standing behind my Zen teacher, Cheri Huber, who had led the retreat. She was purchasing a package of cookies. They were round and smooth and slightly puffy, with a dark chocolate coating, and resembled (I realized later) Zen meditation cushions. But what I saw was the marshmallow cookies of my childhood. If ego had a heart, mine would have broken in that moment. *Chocolate-covered marshmallow cookies?* What true Zen teacher would eat anything so *sweet,* so *soft,* so *childish,* so—*un-Zen?*

Food—or our ideas about it—is a topic addressed in the first part of this book. The simple acts of eating, sleeping, working, and interacting with others can be associated with anxiety and regret, or resentment and envy, or any number of unhappy feelings. In Buddhism, such ordinary dissatisfactions are encompassed by the term "suffering." The perspective Cheri offers in her teaching shifts our attention from the suffering itself to the process by which we cause ourselves to suffer. In the talks presented here, she shows how depriving ourselves will never result in spiritual freedom, while simple kindness to ourselves leads directly to compassion for all.

—

Sweetness is not a quality we tend to associate with Zen. Zen has a reputation for being a rigorous, rather macho pursuit, the spiritual equivalent of boot camp. It is easy in Zen practice to focus on hardship, the discomforts and doubts that arise in long hours of sitting and working meditation. Indeed, among Zen students, one often hears rueful comments to the effect that, yes, indeed, suffering exists.

The existence of suffering is the first of the Buddha's Four Noble Truths. The second is the understanding that suffering is caused by our attachment to an illusory sense of self. The Third Noble Truth asserts that freedom from suffering is possible, and the Fourth tells how we find that freedom.

There is a human tendency, it seems, to cling to the truth that suffering exists while ignoring the truth that freedom is possible.

But *ending* suffering is what the Buddhist path is all about. A great strength of Cheri's teaching is her clear, unwavering focus on exactly how to proceed to end our suffering. In the meditation retreats she has been offering for more than twenty years, in her teaching at the Zen monastery she leads in California, in her numerous books and tapes, Cheri spells out that process in ordinary language. This book, based on informal talks given at retreats across the country between 1996 and 1998, is edited to preserve the compelling immediacy of her speech.

Some of the teaching included here sounds far from sweet. Zen practice can be truly hard, in the sense that it can be difficult to comprehend, difficult to undertake, and at times difficult to bear. When we find ourselves confronted with what appear to be overwhelming obstacles, it may be helpful to keep in mind that there is nothing in any deep spiritual practice that our egos will find attractive or easy.

Why, then, would anyone bother with spiritual practice? Because we have some sense, however nebulous, however fleeting, that we are more than our bodies, more than our feelings, more than our egos, and we want to know all of what we are. My aim here is to bring some balance to the image of Zen as hard and tough and daunting, to reveal a deeper, sweeter truth at the heart of this path.

—

The chocolate-covered marshmallow cookies came to symbolize for me what I think of as the hidden sweetness in Zen. Cheri sometimes mentions the sweetness she sees in people who come to her with their suffering. In that context, sweetness suggests purity, in the way we say fresh air is sweet, or spring water is sweet, or music is sweet, or a particular moment is sweet. To me, Zen practice is sweet in just that way. What I most value in what I learn from Cheri is how to be the opposite of tough: unprotected, open, tender, soft, and even, on occasion, sweet.

Sara Jenkins

❧ introduction: having it all ❧

There is nothing in spiritual practice, as I understand it, that stops us from doing anything, stops us from having anything, stops us from being anything. I do not see spiritual practice as a list of rules to limit our lives. That is what egocentricity is.

Egocentricity (or ego; not to be confused with the term used differently in psychology) is the false sense of the self as separate from everything else. Ego depends on rules and beliefs—the conditioning we are given from birth, first by our parents and then by society—in an effort to protect the self. Because egocentricity is based in separateness, it is threatened by the oneness that is sought in spiritual practice. Ego projects its rules and beliefs onto spiritual practice, and we find ourselves fearing that if we pursue meditation, if we develop centered awareness, if we learn to live from our hearts, then we won't be able to sit on the couch and drink coffee and read magazines, we won't be free to go out with our friends, we won't get to enjoy life.

But there is absolutely nothing in spiritual practice like that.

The only thing that will be missing when we are living from our hearts is the suffering. Not that the suffering cannot be there; in our hearts, in the expansive awareness that develops through sitting meditation, there is plenty of room for all of our experience, including suffering. But there will no longer be any confusion that the small, separate, suffering self of egocentricity is who we are.

For example, we can get into a great snit about something, but we do not have to believe that it is real. Not that the great snit is not there, but it is taking place within a larger reality, like a play being performed on a stage. We can watch a play and feel it affect our emotions and thoughts and bodily sensations, but we are not confused that the play is our life; we never lose awareness that it is all happening on a stage and that at some point it will end and we will stand up and walk out of the theater. In the same way, we can recognize the snit as a very compelling illusion. We know that previously that snit would have taken us over completely, and for some period of time, we would have been so thoroughly identified with that perspective that the snit would constitute our entire reality. But once we enter sincerely into spiritual practice, those days are behind us, because we begin to see through the illusion.

Compassionate awareness is who we really are. Compassionate awareness is what is there when we stop identifying with the conditioned ideas of ourselves. Compassionate awareness was there before all of that; it will be there after all of that is gone; it is there in between all of that. Every time there is a gap in the internal voices of our conditioning, we slip into compassionate awareness.

Every time we stop and turn inward, turn from distraction and suffering to find compassion for ourselves, it is there. Making that turn again and again develops a faith that is based on experience—not a pie-in-the-sky, Pollyanna-ish thing, but a deep knowing from our life experience that everything that happens is our best opportunity to awaken and to end suffering.

Each one of us can immediately have that faith by simply turning around and looking back at our past. We have come up against all sorts of terrible things, and somehow we got through them and came away with greater clarity, kindness, understanding, love. Each time, it is so painful, it is almost unbearable, we believe we won't survive, and then, poof—we pop out of it, and we are strengthened by it. At this point in our lives, we can recognize that process and accept that it is always going to work that way: going into difficulty is the only way through it. No matter how terrifying the next piece of suffering that we come up against, we can have faith that the process of facing it, questioning it, and working with it will bring us precisely what we need to continue our journey.

This practice does not ask us to give up anything. In my own life, I have let go of a great deal, but I have never given up anything. The letting go happens when there is something I want more than whatever it is that I am clinging to. In fact, this practice gives me everything I ever wanted.

Cheri Huber

🪷 1 being in a body 🪷

The suffering the Buddha referred to is readily seen in our attitudes toward our bodily form. Disease, death, and separation from those we love present major occasions for suffering. Daily dissatisfactions arise in our concerns about physical comfort, personal appearance, and how our possessions, surroundings, actions, and interactions with other beings do or do not provide the kinds of experiences we want for ourselves.

We learn those attitudes through the subtle process of social conditioning that prescribes right and wrong, good and bad, acceptable and unacceptable—all based on the egocentric assumption that each of us is a self separate from everything else. But such separateness is an illusion, and that illusion is the source of suffering.

what the mind does, what the body does

Here is my encouragement: do not worry about what is going on in your mind. Let your mind do whatever it does. It is easier to just accept that minds do what they do than to spend your energy searching for the deactivation switch.

A big part of what minds do is draw us into trying to get them not to do what they do. You check in with your mind, your thoughts are all over the place, and you feel upset. "Here I am on a meditation retreat," you think. "It's perfectly quiet, no distractions, no interruptions, and still I cannot quiet my mind."

But that is another thought. Let it go. The mind is just doing its thing, thinking away. What fuels the thinking is your belief in it.

See if you can turn your attention away from the mind and to the body. Become aware of the *hara*—your center, in the belly, where the breath moves the abdomen. Feel your body breathing. Feel it expanding and contracting, expanding and contracting. No expectations; you are not trying to change anything or get anywhere. Let everything be exactly the way it is, keeping your focus on the hara and letting the breath be as relaxed and open as it possibly can be.

Most of us are so unaccustomed to breathing naturally that the body can hardly accept the breath deeper than a couple of inches below the collarbone. When we allow the body to relax, it will naturally accommodate a fuller breath. We do not make the body breathe. It knows how to breathe, breathing is what it does. We simply allow the breathing to happen.

When we turn attention to the hara, when we allow the attention to rest there, with the breath—there we are. We can call that experience being present, being centered; we can call it ease or relaxation or refuge or peace or compassion. It is not any of those, and it is all of those, and it is far more than those.

We leave that experience to return to the familiar world of thoughts and our conditioned responses to them. In the world of our egocentric conditioning, each of us knows ourselves as a separate being that must make its way through life by constantly comparing, judging, doing—anything to maintain the illusion of its existence. (For short, we refer to this illusion of a separate self as *egocentricity* or *ego,* or *the conditioned sense of self* or just *conditioning.*) In the grips of the egocentric illusion of separateness, we are unsettled, confused, not sure; we think we should do this, we do not want to do that, we wonder what is going to happen.

Then we return our attention to the hara and the movement of breath there, and we are at ease. The mind calms, because there is nothing feeding it. And if we pay attention, we will discover that the practice of hara breathing opens our hearts.

energy and ego

There are two very different forces at play in our lives. One is the life force that animates all, which I call "life living." Then there is a force that feeds off of it, like a parasite, taking life force that is not authentically its own.

That second force is our conditioned sense of ourselves as separate from all that is. That egocentric illusion runs our lives— until we become aware of it and learn how to step free of it. It takes a lot of practice to develop that ability, which is what we do in meditation.

Egocentric conditioning has no energy of its own. It is sustained wholly by our life force. When we are suffering, we can feel our vital energy being drained away into feeling upset or afraid or depressed or resentful. Those are conditioned states, and our conditioning lives in us like a parasite.

When our life force is not going into egocentricity, that vital energy is available for the authentic self. We feel enthusiastic, and there is a sense of ease and well-being. But watch how quickly that well-being is drawn off as egocentricity moves back in, latching onto the energy for its own purposes. Let's say I just had a great meal. "Yeah, but now I need a little something more— candy, maybe, or a drink, or a cigarette." Or, I did a great job on a project at work. "Well, yes, but my boss didn't give me the praise I deserved, and I'm pretty depressed." Or, I kept my commitment to meditate thirty minutes every day for a week. "But I'm still not enlightened or even calm and peaceful. I must not be doing it right. I don't have good concentration. Maybe I should take up something different." Those are the voices of egocentric conditioning. They will never let you rest and just be. They are always urging you to get more, do more, be different.

In Buddhism, an image used for this phenomenon is the "hungry ghost." A hungry ghost has a gigantic belly and a long, thin neck tapering up to a little head with a tiny mouth. The hungry ghost is constantly trying to take enough in through that little mouth to feed its immense belly. That is the dissatisfaction of egocentricity, always pulling at us—"Do this! Want that! What about this other thing?"—in a futile attempt to satisfy an endless hunger. If we pay attention to that process in ourselves, we will see that it is pretty much a full-time occupation.

Because the hungry ghost of egocentricity feeds off of the energy of suffering, struggling to stop it will never work; the struggle just creates more of that energy. If egocentricity can get us into a battle with it, it is fat and happy. What it cannot stand is being ignored. In meditation, we practice not engaging with ego—we observe how we are conditioned, but we do not react from that conditioning. That experience builds confidence and courage and faith that we can learn to see life for ourselves and not just through conditioned reactions.

When egocentricity is threatened, though, be prepared for it to raise the stakes and threaten you back. For example, when you begin to practice meditation, ominous thoughts may appear in your head. "If I sit here another minute, my knee will be permanently damaged." Or, "This is probably a cult. My life may be in danger." Or, "I ought to be off this cushion and putting in overtime at work so I can afford nursing home insurance in case I am totally incapacitated. . . ."

In meditation we become aware of how we buy into our egocentric conditioning, how we unconsciously collude with it. By bringing egocentricity out in the open, we begin to see through it, to disengage from it and stop feeding it with our life force.

We can learn a lot about ourselves by observing how popular culture feeds the hungry ghosts with the energy of turmoil and upset. So many movies are designed to terrify us or disgust us or push us to some extreme or other. Turn on the news, and we see the same process on a smaller budget: sights and sounds that stir up energy, manipulate energy. An incident is reported, and we feel agitated in response. Then, as our interest begins to wane, the next thing is presented for us to focus on and get upset over.

Much more important to observe is how that process happens inside our heads. Imaginary scenes, complete with voices and images, take us out into the future or back into the past and produce predictable emotional responses. As soon as one scene fades, along comes the next thing to get stirred up about.

In case you are wondering if this is a crackpot notion from a Californian who took a wrong turn, let me point out that it is actually part of what the Buddha taught, as an explanation for what goes on in this life we are living. Craving and grasping at one experience after another is part of an endless cycle of dissatisfaction. The Buddha described the cycle in detail, and you can observe it within yourself. Watch how energy shifts within you, how you are taken to a point of upset; then your attention attaches to something else, and you are taken to another point of upset, on and on through the day. Notice how that pattern of energy building and dissipating recurs more or less constantly in your life.

In a very different way, meditation also builds energy. When you leave a retreat, even though nothing much seems to have happened, you may realize that you have a high level of energy. Then watch how that energy is dissipated. Notice that when you feel a lot of energy in your body, you start looking for things to do with it. Notice how often that turns into something that is upsetting—feeding the hungry ghost. That process is very useful to look at, to get to know, because it unconsciously drives a great deal of our lives. As we become more aware of it, we can choose not to submit to its manipulation. Then we are free to experience the natural energy of simply being alive.

between deprivation and indulgence

How do we find the compassionate middle way between the extremes of self-deprivation and self-indulgence? Another way of saying that is, how do we make choices that are not determined by messages from our egocentric conditioning?

If I am completely focused on eating, say, here is how I might work with that. I can take a little bit of what is available, eat it slowly, and see what I want afterward. Once I know what I want, and I know how my body feels because I have taken time to be aware of that, then I proceed from there—with an attitude of compassion for whatever aspects of myself are making whatever choices. The approach is one of gentle acceptance, not parental control. If part of me feels, "Okay, now I'm ready to fill up my plate again," responding with, "No, you've had enough!" is not helpful.

For many people, it is easy to idealize a decision not to eat more as the "right" spiritual thing to do. But that is a quick way to move into egocentricity. "Now I've got the answer" reinforces the idea of a separate self, whereas "What is this experience?" opens us to all that is.

Sometimes it is good to eat a lot. If we consciously decide at a certain meal to eat a lot, is "a lot" too much? What was too much at some other time may be just the right amount now.

Egocentric conditioning thrives on deprivation. Then, when we get far enough over into deprivation, the pendulum swings to indulgence, which, of course, puts ego in charge once again. What we aim for on this path is the middle way that is most compassionate to all the parts of ourselves who are involved: the part who always wants more, the part who is critical of that, the part who makes deals about it, the part who gets frustrated and despairing. This is what the Buddha taught—the middle way that allows us to embrace the extremes of deprivation and indulgence, without clinging to either of them.

The secret to the whole thing is that it is not *what;* it is *how.* It is not what we are eating, it is the attitude we bring to it. God, as far as I know, never declared that sugar is bad for you, and, recent research notwithstanding, forcing yourself to eat broccoli at every meal might not be a great idea. When we make decisions, about eating or anything else, with an attitude of kindness and acceptance toward ourselves, with awareness of what is involved in our choices, the conflict between deprivation and indulgence ceases to exist.

recipe for suffering

A large part of our conditioning consists of unexamined belief systems. As we practice meditation, we begin to notice that we hold strong beliefs about all sorts of things, based on nothing more than having been told that they are true.

An interesting belief system to question is about sleep. One day you have not had enough sleep, but you feel wide awake. Another day you have had plenty of sleep, and you are drowsy all day, so you decide you had too much sleep. The next day you have had just the right amount of sleep, and you feel great, so you say, "See? There!" The following day, however, you have had the right amount of sleep and feel awful.

Imagine figuring out the right kind of sheets and pillows and the right kind of blankets on the right kind of bed in the right place in the right room at the right temperature. After eating the right amount of food, you sleep for the right number of hours and then you feel a way you like to feel. What have you gained? Even if you got it all exactly the same way again, you would not feel the way you felt before. You could spend the rest of your life in misery by trying and failing to recreate that experience.

Let's say that in the middle of a normal day, all I can think about is how sleepy I am. I may suspect that it is a conditioned reaction that makes me believe I want to sleep, but everything in me still says, "No, no, I really have to sleep." A good way to test that belief is to put on my shoes and a jacket and take a little stroll outside and see what happens. Often just that amount of movement will open me up to something completely different. I may realize I really do not need to sleep right now. And from that realization, I can simply walk away from the conditioned belief system.

Of course, this does not apply only to sleep; we can each plug in our own content. It is the *process* that is a recipe for suffering: having an idea and clinging to it, having an experience and clinging to it. It seems so important to us to know how we feel and figure out why we feel that way and how we can control life so we will feel the way we like to feel. That is what we mean by "clinging" and "attachment." All these moments are passing when we could simply be alive, but we are lost in trying to figure out how we feel—as if knowing how we feel would add to the quality of our lives. (In most cases, we may have noticed, it detracts.)

Do we really need to keep mental charts so we can know if we are right in our beliefs about why we feel the way we feel? We will ignore all sorts of information that does not support our beliefs, waiting for that one little piece that does, so we can say, "See, that shows I'm right." And what purpose is served by that belief system? It strengthens ego.

As the old Zen saying goes, "Eat when hungry, sleep when tired." The body can be trusted to take care of itself in that way. It is only our conditioned ideas that make it seem that there is a problem. Why not just feel the way we feel?

rewards

At the end of the day, the tendency is to reward ourselves for working hard by going unconscious. We get home and turn to the television or newspaper or whatever will take us away from the present. For many of us, along with that goes eating more than we planned to eat, and usually more of the "wrong" thing, and/or having a few drinks.

When we go to bed and review the day, our conditioned beliefs will be ready with a lot of judgments—basically, a list of what is wrong with us. Then, we go through the promises that tomorrow is going to be different: we will be careful about what we eat, we will be more aware, et cetera. And the next night, there we are in bed making the same kind of deals again.

When we attempt to reward ourselves by going unconscious, we sink into that downward spiral, and the result is anything but feeling refreshed and rejuvenated. On the other hand, if we come home and do some exercise and sitting meditation, we do feel refreshed and rejuvenated. Then we can move into the evening hours feeling that we have done well and had a good day.

Being unconscious does not nurture us, in the same way that sleeping when we are not tired and eating more than we want never nurtures us. Once we know that, we can conclude each work day with something that truly feels good—to our hearts, not to egocentricity.

There is nothing about this practice that is a "should," except that we should pay attention. We can go right on doing whatever we do, but paying as close attention as we possibly can. Then we will know for ourselves that taking time off from awareness will never get us what we want. As we become more aware of how we operate, it becomes harder and harder to convince ourselves that unconsciousness is much of a reward.

being tired and feeling good

Being tired can feel really good. We used muscles, which felt good, and now we can rest them, and that feels good. The muscles are going to get stronger, and that feels good. We can enjoy all that instead of wanting it to be different.

If we believe we are "out of energy," we can try to get energy from somewhere outside ourselves, or we just have to wait until it magically reappears. Is there an alternative? Even when the energy magically reappears, it has to come from some place. We have been talked into thinking that our energy level has to do with sleep, with food, with being in the right places and around the right people under the right circumstances. But those things have nothing to do with finding the wellspring of energy that exists in each of us. Once we discover that wellspring in ourselves, we can experience that energy any time.

Exploring exactly what it means to be tired can reveal the part of the personality that holds in place a belief about tiredness. What is it about being tired that I don't like? What are my underlying beliefs about it? That I am going to fall over? That I am going to die? That I won't be able to lift my arm, won't be able to walk? And what are the implications in my life of holding such beliefs? How do those beliefs limit me?

Someone told me about doing a simple task that involved just two movements and what a joyful experience it was. She realized that it was joyful because her attention was fully focused on what she was doing. What would happen if we focused our attention on the feeling we label "tired?" We might have the same sort of joyful experience simply by being absolutely present to the sensations in the body—and that in itself might generate energy. In any case, without a label, those sensations would no longer be perceived as tiredness.

The key is attention. When we hear ourselves thinking that we are tired, that is a great opportunity to find out what that means. What was the signal that told us we were tired? Where in the body is that little knot of tiredness in which energy is being held? That knot of energy, the place of tightness, is ego's resistance to what is happening, based on a belief about tiredness. When we don't attend to it, that knot of energy fuels the thought pattern, the emotional reaction, and the conditioned behavior patterns that go with it. First is the thought, "I'm tired," then the emotion, "I don't like feeling this way," then the conditioned response, "I want to lie down and read/watch a movie/get something to eat"— whatever it is for each of us. Once the resistance to our experience is released, all that energy is freed up.

If you are sitting in meditation, for example, and your eyes feel tired, take your attention there and see if you can pin down the sensation itself. Is it in one eye or the other or both? Is it in the lid? What exactly is the sensation? Go right to the heart of it, hold it in your awareness. Pretty soon it frees up, and you feel fine.

Then, something else will arise. You turn your attention to one knot of conditioned reactions, and when it goes away, you move on to the next sensation, and then to the next. In sitting meditation, your back hurts. Where? Direct attention to that spot, and the pain dissolves. Then there is discomfort in the neck. Breathe into it, and it releases. You can follow your conditioning around in your body, like connect-the-dots, through the spots where you experience resistance.

You may discover in yourself a belief that can be used as a reason not to question what it means to be tired. For example, you may believe that if you find a knot of energy and release it and then no longer feel tired, you won't be allowed to go home and rest; it's the idea that if you look energetic, somebody may give you another job. That is like believing that if you accept everything, you will never get what you want. We prefer to leave the belief system unexamined in the hope that we will get to relax back into our familiar coping mechanisms.

The reality is that those coping mechanisms do not work; they do not make us happy. If not examining egocentric conditioning meant that at the end of the day we got to do something that made us blissfully happy, I would say don't ever examine any of it. In fact, not examining it keeps us in the cycle of wanting to escape from suffering, doing things to escape, and never feeling any better. As we get older, living with our belief systems does not improve our lives, and our resistance to changing them becomes more rigid. But when we examine the conditioning, when we take it out of that habit realm, then everything becomes possible.

dissolving the problem

The split between mind and body is analogous to the split between the "big I" of oneness and the "small I" of the separate self. The mind is pure, elevated, transcendent, we think, whereas the body is this slothful, sinful heap we drag around until we are liberated by death, which none of us wants to face. Similarly, we are conditioned to believe that the "small I" of egocentricity is the problem. The "big I" of nonseparateness is considered preferable; that is what we are striving for.

But what if what we are seeking is at-one-ness with the "small I" and the "big I" simultaneously? What if it is not either/or, it is nonseparation *within* us, which includes all that we are?

If we were in a tradition that talks about God, I might put it this way. People conjure up a big God of ultimate power and goodness and authority, then they let God off the hook. God supposedly created this mess we live in, yet somehow it is our job to clean it up. God's role, it can appear, is merely to look down a godly nose in disapproval at our puny efforts to do something about the situation. But what would be the point of creating a flawed product and then cutting it loose to try to perfect itself? What is this distance between God and us, this disconnection?

That is, what happens if we question the idea that the inadequate "small I" needs to be corrected and improved and transcended? What if it is not a matter of leaving the "small I" behind and becoming identified with the "big I," not a matter of transcending the body and becoming pure mind?

What if this separation of body and mind does not exist? What if complete identity between "small I" and "big I" is the solution we are looking for?

What if the whole "problem" is an illusion? What if the solution is to be found *within* the "small I," in getting to know it and accept it in total compassion—and the whole time we have mistaken the solution for the problem?

in the moment, in the body

On meditation retreats, it often feels as if we are really present, in our own lives, in our bodies. The body lives in the moment. It is good to remember that, because if we want to know how to get into this moment, the fastest, easiest way is to bring the attention to the body. The body is always right here, right now.

It is the conditioned mind that works so hard to be in some other time and place, constantly dragging us back into the past or out into the future. Bringing the attention into the body and following the breath and living in the moment produces resistance in egocentricity; we can just expect that.

Meditation retreats are designed to produce that conditioned resistance and bring it into awareness. At our retreats, the guidelines are to not speak, not read or write, not make eye contact or watch other people; to participate fully and stick to the schedule; not to do anything other than practice bringing the attention back to the body, back to the breath, back to the present moment. Resistance manifests when we suddenly find ourselves wanting not to be on retreat. That may be expressed in a variety of ways, from slightly bending the guidelines to desperately planning our departure. Egocentricity says, "I don't like all these guidelines. I don't like being told what to do. This morning I feel like sleeping in. I don't want to do any clean-up tasks. I'm tired of paying attention. I want to be distracted." Sometimes making lists is enough to entertain us; other times a nice sexual fantasy will do the trick. If ego is really frantic, we may decide to do something like saying nonsense syllables to ourselves just to get through another half hour of sitting on the cushion. All that is resistance, and resistance is the work of egocentricity.

Here is a different perspective. Whereas in regular life we can feel pulled by a lot of different choices, on retreat it is so wonderfully simple. What do the guidelines say? Keep the silence. So, that is what we do. What does the schedule say? Sitting meditation in fifteen minutes. So, that is what we do. When it is one o'clock and the schedule says rest period, we can debate about where to take our rest and whether to rest lying down, sitting, or standing up, but those are the only choices. It is not a wide-open situation in which we can get caught up on phone calls or write letters or read. No: during that period, we just rest. The part of us that normally drives us through life now gets to take a back seat. We may notice, however, that that part of us is ready and eager to jump back into the driver's seat at any moment, and it will try, and it will succeed. But when we notice that happening, we have the support of simply going back to the schedule, in the same way that we bring attention back to the body, back to the breath.

It may seem as if egocentricity is on our side, that those voices of resistance are concerned for our welfare. But as soon as we catch on to the fact that those very voices are not our salvation but the *source of our suffering,* we begin to find the willingness to distance ourselves from them. Ego tries to lead us off on some scheme to make things better or some distraction or flight of fancy, but we find the willingness to drop all that and bring our attention back to the breath, drop it and come back to the breath, again and again. It is difficult. Our egocentric conditioning is so pervasive, so firmly rooted, that it can feel as if it has been around longer than we have. What we practice is finding the willingness to come back to the breath *anyway* and to merely observe everything that arises to take us out of the moment.

So, a meditation retreat is very supportive of who we really are and extremely threatening to our conditioned idea of ourselves. In most of our lives, egocentricity is in charge. On retreat, we have an environment in which the heart—our true nature, the gentle self, the self that is not separate from all that is—has an opportunity to be supported and allowed to exist fully, at least for a period of time. While we are sitting on the cushion or doing a work project or whatever, it may not seem that it is leading to anything. And, yet, when we leave, we often find that something almost magical happened to us while we were not doing very much, while we were trying to find the willingness to simply follow the schedule and come back to the breath.

other beings

I t is important to seek *sangha,* or spiritual community. Not as a social network, not getting together with people because they remind us of our spiritual path, but to actually sit together, to be silent together, to offer each other, through our presence, the encouragement to practice.

When it is somebody else's turn to set up the cushions and ring the bells for a group sitting, and you would like to stay home and take it easy, instead of succumbing to that, it is important to make the effort to show up because you know that person is making the effort. Rising to the occasion in that way, we do for the love of others what we would not be willing to do for ourselves—until we realize that we are doing it for our own true nature, which is all that is.

Of course, there is a whole other aspect of sangha. Someone told me about an interview with a Christian monk who had been in the monastery for a long time. The interviewer asked what was the most difficult part of monastic life. The monk thought for a while, then he said, "Well, I guess I'd have to say it's the other monks."

Isn't it true for all of us? There are times on retreat when we are convinced that the other retreatants are the most wonderful people on the face of the earth, and we feel so blessed to spend this precious time with them. Other times we wonder if most of them were rounded up from some institution. But it is good to remember that just as we are annoyed by others, so are we annoying to them.

Dealing with other people can be annoying and illuminating at the same time. Out in the world we are taught that we can see something outside ourselves that has nothing to do with us. For example, we see somebody do something that is outside our belief system, related to sexuality, say. We cannot recognize the potential in us for doing that same thing because of our belief that people who do that are bad. Instead of acknowledging that potential in ourselves and our beliefs about it, we deal with our discomfort by saying that the other person is wrong. Understanding that kind of projection is crucial. Projection is a powerful tool used by egocentricity to constantly reinforce the sense of separateness.

In this practice, we are encouraged to bring everything back to ourselves—because there is nothing going on but oneself. Everything we project out onto other people we can follow back to see in ourselves, the good, the bad, and the ugly. I look outside myself, I see somebody doing something, and I put a label on it. If I am aware of projection, I will own that quality myself. Whatever that person is doing, whatever label I have given it, whatever I think it means, I bring all that back inside and admit that I know nothing about that other person, only about myself. All the things I think I know have come from inside me, and I am putting them out onto others. In that way, other people are very useful in the development of our own self-knowledge.

So, great gratitude for sangha, for those of us who practice together, who reflect for us a good clear view of who we are. We are one another's best spiritual opportunities.

impermanence

There is no advantage in becoming attached to a spiritual teacher as a person in a particular bodily form. If we are too focused on the teacher and then something happens to the teacher, that might be the end of our practice. In the case of someone like Mother Teresa, we can suspect that people are not so much attracted to the spiritual practice she represented as they are attached to an idea of her. That confuses the process with the form. The practice is what is important; the forms come and go.

Most people I work with recognize that they know almost nothing about the person Cheri. They have their thousands of projections, of course, but little actual information. When you look at the person who sits in the front of the room, whether it is me or one of the monks, what you see is the practice. You might see a centered quality, which is an expression, in a particular form, of what it is like to live in moment-to-moment awareness. Seeing that helps you learn to recognize it in yourself.

That process has nothing to do with me as a person. If the thought comes through your mind, "I don't think what Cheri said came from a centered place," awareness of projection would cause you to stop and consider that the point is not whether it came from a centered place in someone else but to check what is going on within you.

It is like looking into a mirror: you look at me, and you see yourself. That is the agreement we have in personal guidance interviews and also in group discussions. When we come together to talk, you do not say, "Well, Cheri, how's life?" and I say, "Well, Jack, I'll tell you, I've been . . . ." When you come to talk to me, we are going to talk about what is happening with you. You can know that in a guidance interview (or discussion) you do not have to have a personality, you do not have to be cute, charming, clever, bright, or anything else. You can be exactly as you are at that moment, and that will be mirrored for you.

There is a stage in spiritual practice when you will be able to turn your attention fully to your heart when we are together, but when you go back home, you get caught up in life, conditioning takes over, and pretty soon everything is being run by egocentricity again. You may conclude from that that you need to go somewhere to be with the teacher again, because the teacher has the secret, the answer. No: all the teacher has is the ability to mirror back to you who you are. It is simply that the places where you see me—retreats, workshops, the monastery—are safe places for you to have that experience within yourself, to see what is being mirrored. The way it works is that being in proximity to the practice, as embodied in people who are pursuing it full time, helps you to recognize the practice in yourself and to deepen it in yourself. It is not that when I go away from where you are, the practice goes away too. Your job is to become more and more yourself, then increasingly the connection is not broken when we are not together. The feeling of connectedness grows—connectedness not only with the teacher but also with the sangha, with all those who have gone before on this path.

When this person Cheri dies, whatever of the practice is internalized in you will go on. You will have that as an experience to turn to as your reference point. Then the work will be to see that experience in other places and other people and to continue to recognize it in yourself.

⚛ 2 identity ⚛

The crucial illusion that we aim to see through in Buddhist practice is our mistaken sense of our own identity. Conditioned to believe that we are separate from and in many ways pitted against the rest of existence, we suffer unnecessary loneliness, fear, and greed. As we turn our attention to those egocentric beliefs, we can see through the illusion they create. Beyond—and even within—the uniqueness of our personalities, we discover a new identity of oneness with all, in which nothing is lacking, everything is available, and our true nature is seen to be goodness.

who you are

The Buddha talked about our true nature being eternal. Our true nature is what has our best interest at heart, not in a specific personal way, but as general well-being. Whatever is hateful, angry, vindictive, miserable; whatever is self-pitying; whatever seeks something for itself at someone else's expense—that is not our true nature. What is present, what is aware, what is compassionate, what has the nature of interconnectedness and affinity and empathy—a knowing that what is hard for us is hard for everybody, that we do not deserve more or less than anybody, that we are all in this together, and really there is only one of us, which is all that is—that is who we really are.

In any moment, we can tell which reality we are living in, true nature or egocentricity. Our spiritual work is to learn to discern the difference between them and increasingly to choose the authentic self.

There is no reason to believe that people who are doing spiritual practice are better than, or better off than, people who are not doing spiritual practice. It is just that for some of us, there is a longing we must work to satisfy in the same way we previously might have worked to get ahead in business or buy a bigger house. Once that course is set, there is no turning back. In our hearts we know there is a place of ease and comfort regardless of circumstances, and that is where we are headed.

The path of conscious awareness is no bed of roses, however. It is difficult for everybody; that is something we have to face. We may not always be willing to receive the kindness that is there; we cannot always experience what happens in our practice as compassion. When we are in the middle of learning a hard lesson about our own selfishness or arrogance, it does not feel like compassion. Having an attachment ripped from deep in our being does not feel kind. Yet when it is gone, when the wound is healing, we can see that the process was one of pure compassion.

The Buddha used this image: if there is a knife in you, it is compassionate to pull it out. Pulling it out is going to be terrifying and it is going to hurt, but you are not going to live with the knife in there. Your best chance is to pull it out as quickly as possible and get on with the healing.

Meanwhile, it can be helpful to remind yourself about who you truly are. You are not your body. You are not your mind. You are not your emotions. You are not your ego. Your true nature is goodness, and it is eternal.

narrowing the field of identities to none

When we start out, we may bring to everything the same ability to suffer. As we begin to see through our conditioning in places, to see how it operates in certain areas of life, we may get to the point where we can experience joy in, say, working meditation. We have let go of the identity—the conditioned pattern of relating to the world—that believed it had to hate anything called work. But when it comes to a relationship, we still get stuck in suffering. Our beliefs about ourselves in relationship are just as convincing as ever, which is to say, we are still identified with that particular suffering part of ourselves. Then, when we see through that belief system, that identity, there will be something else to suffer over. Egocentricity, which is constituted of such identities, is all too eager to offer up another one, because to be without such identity means death to ego.

For a long time, we continue to believe that the suffering is caused by something out there—a job, a person, money, children, health, meditation practice. When we look deeper, though, we see that in all those different situations, to which we bring a whole array of identities, we ourselves are the single common element. That is, it is not the content of the suffering that is the point but a *process* of suffering that is maintained within us.

As we see through more and more of our identities, the pieces of content that we have not seen through become ever more important. If we had only one piece of life left in which we continued to believe that the content was really the cause of our suffering, and that piece stayed at the same level of importance as when it was one among many, what might happen? It might just drop away. Then we would have nothing to suffer over, nothing to maintain our identity with. So that last piece of content can seem really important, really real. Our whole existence can be taken over by our identification with that issue and our suffering over it.

At that point, we have narrowed the field of identities to one. And there is nothing left but to take that terrifying last step: allowing that final identity to dissolve. At which point, suffering is no more, because there is no one left to suffer.

dissatisfaction guaranteed

If you want to make sure you always have an identity, choose a goal that is unattainable. Let's say the only thing you want is to know when you are centered, meaning that you are present to what exists in each moment rather than caught up in conditioned thoughts about what might be. Since we cannot know when we are centered—because the "I" of ego does not exist in the experience of being centered—if that is the only thing you want, your experience of life is guaranteed to be unsatisfactory.

What we identify as "I" wants all moments to have something consistent about them, so it can cling to rules about how to be. But that is not how life is. We think if we could know for sure who we are and how to be, then we could relax. In fact, we cannot know those things, and we conclude that our only option is to feel discomfort. But it is good to question that conclusion. Can you see that some part of you wants there to be a problem, wants the discomfort? That aspect of ego is maintained by the process of dissatisfaction. As long as you are dissatisfied, you *do* know who you are: you are someone who is uncomfortable.

We need only one dissatisfaction in life to keep identity alive. It can be a single deep and abiding dissatisfaction, or it can be a sequence of changing dissatisfactions. It does not matter; both accomplish the same thing.

When you have been doing spiritual practice for a while, it can be shocking to realize that you are at the point where you could end suffering, and now you have to decide if you want to. That such a thing might happen occurs to almost no one ahead of time. We think that of course we want to end suffering. If we admitted that we didn't want to end suffering, what might happen to us? It's a deep down, primitive, appeasing-the-gods sort of thing: we have to say we want to end suffering, because if we admit that we don't, we may get some real suffering.

Wanting to suffer is actually quite common, and, from an ego-centric point of view, quite understandable. Suffering guarantees us a certain amount of attention. It can serve as an excuse not to do things we are afraid to do. It can bind other people to us. It gives us something to do, someone to be. The absence of suffering would leave a great unknowable void in our lives.

If we discover that we want to suffer, it is easy to feel horrified, to plunge into despair. "I want to suffer—I am really hopeless!" Well, does all of me want to suffer? No. If that were the case, I wouldn't bother practicing meditation. What are the parts of me that do not want to suffer? And what are the parts that do?

Once we see clearly the parts of us that do want to suffer, perhaps it is time to take our lives out of their clutching, clinging fingers. They can go along for the ride, but they don't need to steer.

who knows?

Something in our hearts draws us to want to be as compassionate and centered as we can be. From that same motive, we can want to know if what we are doing is harmful or harmless, if a given action leads toward suffering or away from suffering.

We may feel completely justified in wanting to know whether what is operating in us is the heart or the ego—and that may be something we cannot know. "But I need to know!" we say. That little note of urgency is a clue that the question is not coming from clarity of mind, from present-moment awareness, from the heart. When wanting to know the answer becomes more important than compassion, a crucial shift takes place, the shift back into egocentric conditioning.

A good place to start exploring this is with the question, who needs to know? The answer is, a part of ourselves that is separate from the situation, that has something to gain from the knowledge, like using it to maintain a certain sense of self. Only that part of us would have a need to know.

In wondering what is guiding us, whether we are listening to the heart or the ego, it is important to stay alert to the process going on within us. Are we striving for a certainty that we know who we are and which answer will lead us toward compassion and away from suffering? Or are we slowly—and we cannot leap to this place I am pointing to—realizing that there is no one to know the answer to that question? Are we gradually dissolving the illusion of being someone who can and should know such things?

We may "know" the right answer, in the sense that people say to me, "I understand the problem, I see the ego in it, but I'm still suffering." They have not taken the step yet into that intuitive sensing that *there is no problem.*

Yes, the answer is that there is no problem. We may "know" that answer, but we cannot live it until we know it inside the marrow of our bones. That is what is meant by the encouragement to pursue our spiritual practice as if our very life depends on it. We have to go after what we are seeking with everything in us, non-stop—knowing that approaching it that way will drive it further away from us, and knowing that if we stop, it will be utterly unavailable to us. We have to pursue it in that wholehearted manner until there is nothing left of us to pursue it. And then there will only be what we are seeking.

pursuing the life of the heart

People talk about the heart opening as if that means instant transformation into saintliness. But the heart opening might be quite a bit less dramatic. It could be something as simple as a flicker of what we interpret as doubt, like thinking, "Well, maybe there could be something to all that meditation stuff." For a split second, we were not lost in maintaining an egocentric identity that is skeptical about spiritual practice. When there is even a tiny opening, we can dive right into it.

In that moment, if we step out of one identity—one aspect of egocentric conditioning that establishes our separate selfhood—and there is nothing to focus on right then, we might spend some time sort of free-floating around. Quickly, however, most of us will float right over into another identity. We focus our attention on the breath because it is much easier to have something to come back to, whether it is sensing the expansiveness of the body as we breathe, or an experience in the body that feels like "center," or a feeling of relaxation, or just not resisting anything. As we keep turning our attention to that experience, it seems to grow larger.

What in the beginning is just a fleeting hint of peace or well-being becomes recognizable when we encounter it again. Now we are going to start actively looking for it. Days, weeks, months, years may go by, but we know that once when we were sitting in meditation, there was that little moment of clarity, like a coming to, a waking up, and for a split second we were in a different reality.

We begin tracking it down, like a dog following a trail. We may be told that searching for it, chasing it, trying to grab hold of it will push it away, but that does not matter. We are pursuing it anyway.

And—there it is again! Days, weeks, months, years may go by, but now it has happened twice. Now we are in hot pursuit of that experience. Sometimes we are aware of just a faint trace of it, like a feeling left over from a dream, a memory of a different reality. Each time we get a glimpse of it, it grows larger and clearer. Once it gets big enough, we realize that we have actually known the experience for a long time; many people say they recall it from childhood.

When we recognize the experience clearly, and we know that it feels better to be in that place than anywhere else, resistance really kicks in. That is the first time when being present to ourselves seriously threatens egocentric survival structures. In recognizing that place where we want to be, we are saying that we are willing to give up the structures of conditioning in order to be there. Egocentricity's response is, "Now, wait a minute, you're going too far." Then the spiritual battle begins in earnest. Ego pulls out all the stops; it even makes promises. "Okay, we can negotiate. You can have a better life if you just stick with us. We can work on this."

We have been seduced by those voices over and over again. Lying on the couch watching sitcoms was not all we hoped it would be, so we tried the next thing ego presented, and that failed, and the next thing failed, and one by one the things that our conditioning has to offer us have been checked off the list. We finally meet the love of our life, and even that, it turns out, does not provide nonstop well-being for us, does not keep us from feeling frightened or alone or anxious or insecure, especially when we consider that that person could leave or die.

Finally we get it: egocentricity can pull off a lot of fascinating stuff, but it has nothing to offer who we truly are. It will not be there at our side to comfort us when we wake up at three a.m. worrying that we have a brain tumor, or when we wake up and realize that the person closest to us *did* die. The only thing that can give us what we need and long for is the life of the heart.

held together with habits

To explore the relative merits of holding on and letting go, we do not have to begin by tackling the big issues in our lives. The little things we cling to are great to experiment with. Knowing that clinging could possibly be synonymous with suffering, we might choose one little thing we cling to, then play around with letting it go and see what happens.

For example, if you stopped drinking your habitual cup of Earl Grey tea, you would be a different person. And that is why you do not want to do it. Green tea is said to have an antioxidant effect, which is good for your health in all sorts of ways. You could drink green tea all day long and feel good about yourself; in fact, you would almost be a fool not to drink it! But that is not what you are drinking.

As long as you are drinking something you do not feel good about, there can be this little tension of feeling that you should look at this habit, because you know you should give it up. But you don't want to give it up; you love Earl Grey tea. And you hate yourself for not being able to break the habit. Notice that that one little habit has love, hate, a whole drama, which keeps a piece of identity in place. The aggregate of such habits is what we call "me."

I do not advocate giving things up. If there is any feeling of not drinking Earl Grey tea any longer because it is not good for you and you will be a better person if you don't drink it, it will not work. That is simply moving from one side of the duality to the other, and pretty soon you will be back to the first position. Most of us keep the structures of egocentricity firmly in place: the things we cling to because we desire them, and the things we push away because we fear them. The result is that we stay as we are, with our conditioning intact and unexplored. If there is the willingness to allow everything to be as it is, however, these apparent problems simply fall away.

Letting go of a habit involves cultivating an attitude of mind that wants to see what will happen when a change is made, an attitude that is curious, open, attentive, accepting. Eventually, the habit becomes a non-issue, and you are a different person.

You can break a habit by consciously dissolving that one ego structure. Then you may want to see what it is like to dissolve another one. Just choose a habit and watch. You can feel the identity start to slide a bit.

Once you get beyond the content—the Earl Grey tea—to focus on the process, then you are messing with the latitude and longitude, the deeper structures that tell us what's what. Pretty soon the whole system of conditioned beliefs is having a hard time keeping its orientation. Life starts looking different. You start feeling different. You are different. You are no longer identified with the forms that held your reality in place. Reality itself is going to be different.

old friend

One of the big traps in spiritual practice is thinking that we have finished with some aspect of our conditioning, only to have it reappear much later. If we take that personally, then we are heading right down the trail of suffering. But if we say, "Ah, that again—that's interesting," our relationship with it is completely different.

In long-term spiritual practice, we can find ourselves in this sort of terribly humbling situation. We have been going along feeling quite pleased with our spiritual progress. When we scan the horizon, there is nothing in sight that we have not dealt with. In the whole three hundred and sixty degrees of our egocentric conditioning, we have seen it all, we have worked our way through it, piece by piece. We must be finished! And the next thing we know, we are flattened with the same piece of suffering that drove us to spiritual practice in the first place. Now we are stuck in hell and absolutely powerless to do anything about it. All we can do is hang on and pray we survive.

A big part of the humiliation is that the hell consists of the very same old stuff that we have seen again and again. But being humbled in that way is the best thing that can happen. Otherwise, we might have been deluded into thinking that there was nothing left to do in our practice, and we could have spent a lot of time lost in that delusion. The humbling experience is useful in that now we know we will see that same conditioning again. We will find our way out of the present hell. We will recover from this. We will get to feeling good about life again—and sooner or later that same conditioning will be back. Eventually, we just know that and accept it.

Each time I get slammed with my conditioning, I am so very grateful that it is the same thing over and over again. I would be in big trouble if every time it was something I had never encountered before. It is a good system: one life, one set of karmic conditioning.

For the ego, the reaction can be, "Same old stuff all the time, so boring—where is the drama in that?" Of course, that is a way to get out of examining it.

For the heart, though, having the same old conditioning arise is great. It is familiar stuff, and so it is manageable. It is an old friend who has been around for a very long time and who we can count on for many more visits. The heart has no problem with putting out the welcome mat.

We have absolutely no evidence that we can get somewhere in spiritual practice and then coast the rest of the way. Some people claim to have finished with their conditioning, but often they tend to slide off into strange areas shortly thereafter. So, we can just know our conditioning will be coming around, and that is all right. Our attitude toward it can be friendly acceptance. We can even check in with it periodically. "How are you doing in there? Come see me any time. I'll be ready."

the parable of the eighty rolls-royces

Bhagwan Shree Rajneesh will forever be a hero of mine, because by having eighty Rolls-Royces, he rubbed everybody's noses in their own attitudes about having and not having. To me, it is as if he were saying, "You have this belief system that spiritual people cannot have things. Well, here are eighty Rolls-Royces. Deal with it!" The fact that he did not do anything with all those cars—they just sat there—makes it even worse for some people. If he had driven them around, at least we could know that he was a pleasure-seeking, luxury-craving charlatan. But he just parked them there in a row.

Materialistic America could not deal with it. I wonder if a little part of our resentment is that we do not have even one Rolls-Royce and he had eighty. We like to complain that people are starving, and the man is collecting Rolls-Royces. But if we mentioned that, then we might be obliged to look at what we collect instead of feeding starving people. Still, our own greed is on such a small scale in comparison that we feel justified in focusing on his.

What is behind our attitudes about having and not having? Some people have lots of stuff because that is how egocentricity keeps them from realizing that they do not need anything. Other people have nothing because that is the way egocentricity keeps them from realizing that they are the rightful recipients of all goodness in the world.

The people who cannot allow themselves anything have deprivation as their identity. Deprivation is often associated with spirituality, but as an identity, it is still egocentric; it is still clinging to a belief about how one needs to be in order to feel all right about oneself. As far as I am concerned, clinging to deprivation is not spiritually superior to a belief like, "I've got to have a Rolls-Royce or my life is nothing, and I'm not going to be able to stand it." It is obvious that people with both attitudes are equally stuck in their conditioning.

I would hope that those of us who project onto Bhagwan Shree Rajneesh our own greed and craving and clinging will be helped to recognize that we do not need anything but ourselves to be all right. What we are, in and of ourselves, is all we ever need.

here

Here in this moment is life living, and out there in conditioned thoughts and imagination is an illusion of separateness, an identity—what I like, what I don't like, what I want, what I do— who I am other than all that is. That illusory identity exists outside of life, which is why it is so unsatisfying.

We have moments when we come back here and there is nothing going on, and we are perfectly happy; we are complete. Then we leave that experience to run to this thing and that thing and the next thing, to make our mark or get what we want or be who we think we should be, and we are still unfulfilled.

Then we come back to the present. We are sitting on the cushion or walking along or stopped at a traffic light or whatever. We are just here, there is nothing going on, and everything is fine.

That is what we practice: coming back here. The sense of I/me/mine does not exist when we are here.

what the teacher sees

It is a tricky and dangerous thing to be in the role of spiritual teacher in people's lives. I feel fortunate in that certain attributes make me qualified for the job. The first is that I am an intensely shy, reserved, and private person, easily embarrassed by attention. Being in this role has been and continues to be a challenging part of my own spiritual practice. Second, I am lucky in not being attracted to wealth. If I were forced to drive a Jaguar, I would want to put a sign on it saying, "My real car is a Saturn." There is no particular strength of character in that; it is just a basic personality orientation. Also, there is a way in which this job was foisted on me, and that too makes me well-suited for it. Not that I am a victim in any way, or that I could not walk away from it at any moment, but that I did not seek it. And yet I find tremendous willingness to do it, and I love it.

My teacher used to talk about being an undue influence in people's lives and the fine line that a teacher does not want to cross. He would say, "When you touch the deepest, most intimate part of people, they will want to give you their money, their bodies, whatever they feel is a fair exchange for what you have given them." To be on the receiving end of so many people's ideas that you have what they want, to constantly keep in mind that that has nothing to do with you as a person—that is very difficult. If all your life you wanted to be wonderful and finally somebody says you are wonderful, it can be hard to say, "No, that's really just your projection." You might be forgiven for thinking instead, "Gosh, I'm glad somebody finally noticed!"

We each bring to spiritual practice what we can bring. What I bring in my role as teacher is simply years of experience. From my perspective, the traditional Buddhist image of trying to cross the water to get to the opposite shore falls short as an analogy for the spiritual journey. Crossing water seems much more manageable, frankly, than dealing with egocentric conditioning. I picture it more like a jungle full of land mines and wild beasts and marauders. That is the territory we are trying to traverse, to get to the other side where there is peace and clarity and freedom.

As a person who has gone into that jungle and come out on the other side, and gone back in again and come out again, and even made some trails into it, I can say with some degree of authority that it is terrifying. And it is particularly terrifying if you are going to wander out into it on your own. I would never encourage anybody to do that. It will take everything you have to make it across. But if you learn where to put your feet, what to pay attention to, how to stay with yourself, how to attend and find compassion within yourself, it is possible to make the journey. In fact, it is a lot more than that. It can be fun. It can be thrilling. It is the "master game" compared to which all other pursuits pale in significance.

As a teacher, it is my job to know, when you do not, that you are equal to the journey, that you can do it, that you possess everything you need to get where you want to go. The way you can know that is that you project all those qualities onto the teacher, and it is the teacher's job to mirror them back to you. In that way, you recognize that you are not following someone else, you are following your own true nature. It is just that sometimes it is easier to recognize your true nature in a form other than your own.

On long retreats, I always become aware of how precious— that is the word that comes to mind—how precious people are, how dear, how innocent. Their behaviors in the world may not give any sign of that, but to spend just a moment with somebody when their heart is open, you see that there is only goodness there. Often that happens when they are telling me something they consider awful about themselves. But in the act of revealing that, they reveal their inherent goodness.

To see someone's suffering, even to feel one's own heart break because of that suffering, is one thing. But to assume that something is wrong with another person seems to me disrespectful. I cannot know how a particular situation serves as a spiritual opportunity for somebody else. I must trust that every situation is each person's best opportunity to discover their true nature, which is goodness. That discovery is what is meant in Buddhism by "awakening."

I find it bizarre that in spiritual practice there is wide acceptance of projecting our enlightenment onto someone else, with the implication that that person is enlightened and we are not. There is subtle and not so subtle encouragement to believe that the enlightenment belongs to the other person, and we just happen to be sharp enough to notice it.

The point in becoming aware of projection is not just to get us to own the miserable qualities we attribute to other people. It is primarily to get us to recognize that what we project onto God, onto

Jesus, onto Buddha, onto saints and teachers is also a projection of our own experience. If you find yourself awed by "my" wisdom and clarity, notice whose mind that wisdom appears in. If you are moved by "my" compassion, notice whose body you are feeling it in, notice whose heart is opening.

It is essential that we begin to break down those illusions of separateness. Why, in any spiritual practice, would we want to foster a belief that teacher and student are separate and unequal? Why would we want to perpetuate any illusion of separateness?

I feel that I am the most privileged person in the world because of the relationship I am able to have with people. I see people at their sweetest, most tender, most defenseless. I guess that is why it is hard for me to understand when other people cannot see that goodness is our inherent nature. I get to see it all the time. I spend day after day experiencing the sweetness of human beings. I consider my primary job description to be assisting people to realize that I have given them nothing. I have simply held up a mirror that has helped them see what has always been so.

to save ourselves

The Buddha's last statement is said to have been, in effect, "You must work out your own salvation diligently." How do we do that?

Each person has one person to save—which does not mean beating that person into being what egocentricity says they "should" be. A popular idea, from people who do not know that another possibility exists, is that God said, "Human beings need to be like this, this, this, and this, and you should do whatever you need to do, to yourself or to other people, to be those ways." As a result, we are more focused on what other people are doing than on what we are doing. That is not helpful. It is extremely popular, but it is not at all helpful.

So, we are taught that we must make ourselves be the way we should be. We look at the rules: we should not be lustful. Here we are in human bodies that are, depending on age and hormone levels, burning with lust. But we have gotten the message that if we were the right sort of spiritual person, we would not be having that experience. What, then, do we do with that experience? We hate the part of ourselves who is having it, deny that part of ourselves, punish that part. And because that is what we are taught to do, we are an extremely punitive society. As a society we hold a belief that punishment makes bad people good. Even very smart people believe that at a deep level.

Something may happen that causes us to recognize for a brief moment that there might be another approach, a larger perspective, but that realization is folded quickly into the old belief system. We could come to that larger reality with an attitude like, "Hallelujah, another way is available—let's jump into that ocean of bliss!" Instead, we project standards onto spiritual practice to reinforce our conditioned sense of ourselves: "I should be attentive, and my attention wanders. I should be more aware, but I don't seem to be. I realize that compassion is possible, but I'm not always compassionate." Then we conclude that we are bad and wrong and hopeless after all, and we settle back down into the restricted world of ego.

The moment we drop the illusion of being separate and the idea that things should be different, the entire universe falls into place. It is interesting to consider—and I would challenge everybody to have the experience—what your emotional state would be if you were to drop the illusion of being a separate self. What would anger be like? We assume that if we were to drop a concern about being angry, we would become raving maniacs, endangering ourselves and everyone else. But if we drop the illusion of being separate, what would happen to that whole premise? Even the idea that there is a "you" who should be compassionate precludes the possibility of compassion; compassion is what is there when "you" are not.

All the problems and difficulty exist because we think we are something else, and we are attempting to maintain that identity. My idea is that human beings like to focus on saints and purity and God and goodness and that sort of thing because it maintains the ego structure. Believing in those things sets up the familiar self-hating situation in which we imagine something so wonderful that in comparison we are judged worthless. The essential duality, the essential separation.

If we can get past that recycling of conditioned beliefs, we may realize that everything we have been projecting onto God, Jesus, Buddha, or whatever moved us to see something larger than had been available to us before—that experience is inside us.

Our essential nature—the core of our being, the authentic self—is inherently good. It is goodness. It is not goodness as opposed to badness; it is nonseparation. It is interconnectedness. It is compassion. Once we touch into that, we simply lose all desire to do harmful things to others. When we leave that core of compassion, when we move back into identification with ego-centric conditioning, we are right back in the world of fear, hate, and punishment. Then we come back to the present, we step free of our conditioned reactions, our eyes clear, we are lucid again for a moment. We realize that there is nobody else, there is nothing wrong, there is nothing that needs to be done, nothing that needs to be different. If we were talking in terms of God, we would realize that there is only God. Once we are aware that that is available to us, then the work of spiritual practice is to increasingly move into that reality, to embrace in compassionate acceptance every piece of suffering that we have projected out onto everything else.

Then, the one person we need to save is saved, because a huge confusion has fallen away. We no longer believe that we are that little separate, abandoned, isolated, desperate, inadequate, suffering self. We know that is a case of mistaken identity. What we experience in our deepest moments as our true nature is the intelligent awareness that animates all forms. We return to that awareness, over and over and over again, and each time we do, the compassion expands. It extends to include more and more and more. Eventually, one guesses, there is nothing left but that compassion, and nothing is outside of that compassion.

I say our true nature is goodness only because we have to call it something and words are what we use, with the understanding that words are inadequate. But from my perspective, there needs to be an understanding that the "goodness" that is our true nature includes earthquakes that kill thousands of people. It is not other than that, it is not goodness in the sense of sunshine and happiness and light. It is life, nonseparate from all that is.

If we were to drop the illusion of a separate self, we would not be living ahead of ourselves. We would not be worried. We would not have agendas. We would not know what we are going to do. All of that would fall away, leaving us tremendously vulnerable. And tremendously free.

🪷 3 on the cushion 🪷

Sitting meditation is the heart of Zen practice. Sitting still but alert, with the attention focused on the breath, we can experience awareness of things as they are, including our suffering. In noticing the shift back and forth between simply being present to our experience and then imagining something different, wishing for life to be other than it is, we see how our minds operate in ways that cause us to suffer. We also see how unnecessary suffering is.

what we practice

We must appreciate the irony of sitting in meditation and making a plan to develop awareness at some future time. When we catch ourselves doing that, depending on how disidentified we are from ego, we can chuckle over it. Then we can remember that the best preparation we can make for another time and place is to drop everything else and be present in this moment. Then we do not need a plan. We can have faith that in the moment, whatever is appropriate will be here for us.

A safe place to practice developing that faith is sitting meditation. When we are on the cushion, nothing much is going on except what conditioned mind brings to the experience. We all know how it works: we are right here in the moment, and there is a sense of well-being, clarity, even insight. Then in comes the conditioning, and suddenly things are wrong; we need things to be different; we are off somewhere else.

There are also times when something goes through the mind and there is no need to think about it or compare it to anything or have an opinion about it. We simply let it go. The attention stays with the breath, in peace and clarity. Through repeating that process, we prove to ourselves that when we drop everything and come into this moment, what we need is here. That is what we practice in meditation.

When our attention remains in the present moment, we may be having a painful experience, but probably the pain will be in a larger context than merely what it says about us. That is, rather than leaving the present and taking the pain personally, having it refer back to us—"How can I stand this? What is going to happen to me?"—there is a universal quality to it. When we are fully present to our experience, there is insight about what it means to be alive, what it means to be a human being, what it means to live in compassionate awareness. And all of that is available in every moment.

Most of us are not open to somebody else telling us what our experience is, and yet when egocentricity does that, through those voices in our heads, we accept it without question. A common example is sitting in meditation and believing the voice that tells us that we need to shift position or make a to-do list or even get up from the cushion and do something productive.

It is good to question those voices, just as we would question a voice from outside ourselves. We can just listen and be non-committal, or we can be polite and offer the best line from the entire personal growth movement, "Thank you for sharing that." Whatever our response, it is crucial that we offer it with the attitude that we do not need to be told what our experience is, we are going to find out for ourselves. The point is not to find out what is wrong, which is what those voices have to tell us. The point is to notice what goes on in our minds.

Simply noticing can seem very hard to do. When I give instructions for sitting meditation, I tell people that we sit in a certain posture and turn our attention to the breath, and then we just notice. Almost nobody gets it for a really long time: that is all there is to it—you really do just sit there and simply notice. People report back to me that they cannot get rid of their thoughts, they cannot concentrate, they cannot clear their minds, they cannot do this difficult thing, and they might as well give up. But when was there any mention of getting rid of thoughts or concentrating or clearing the mind? The instructions were to just sit there, attend to the breath, and notice. Not to have theories. Not to have opinions. Most definitely not to make ourselves feel bad: we are learning how to end suffering!

Einstein is said to have observed that a problem cannot be solved by the same mind that created it. And that is what we try to do. We turn our spiritual practice over to egocentricity, and then we wonder why it does not make us happy.

Spiritual practice does not require much from us; we do not have to figure out anything. I would encourage everyone to just show up, with no standards about how spiritual practice should be. The practice itself provides all the standards that we need:

One, sit on the cushion.

Two, sit still.

Three, pay attention.

There is nothing about watching ourselves to make sure we do not do anything wrong. Nothing about monitoring our posture so we can critique our efforts. Nothing about judging ourselves as inadequate if our attention wanders more than our standards say it should. There is none of that—and yet almost everybody who starts meditation practice brings all that right in with them.

It is a big step in the right direction when we can find the willingness to just drop those standards, along with everything else, and do the only thing that matters: turn our attention to the breath, come back to the here and now. Then, when egocentricity appears, we can see it.

recognizing egocentricity

It can happen that you are going along doing your practice, and suddenly you get to a place where you really do not want to be. It can be as simple as you just do not want to be sitting on the cushion. If you have been practicing a while, you will have tools for dealing with that kind of situation, and you can take out your toolbox and open it up and find the right tool for dealing with "I don't want to." But sometimes none of your tools quite fits the particular situation. Nothing works. What you are left with is an unequivocal "No, I don't want to be sitting on the cushion."

What helps me in that kind of situation is to recognize that statement as the voice of egocentricity—and to know that egocentricity is never going to want to meditate. I can just say, "That is egocentricity. Its job is to not want to, and my job is to not believe it. If I wait for egocentricity to get enthusiastic about meditation, meditation is not going to happen."

Another simple intellectual understanding that I find helpful is remembering that only ego fears. If something in you is terrified, you can just know it is egocentricity. The terror is that ego will lose control.

Try to change something, though, and ego resists. It likes the drama of fear or aversion, which positions the separate self firmly at center stage. Anything that interrupts that drama, ego sees as a threat. And meditation interrupts the drama in a big way.

attention residing in awareness

In meditation practice, we are always working to bring attention back to reside in awareness. Our conditioning supports attention that flits from thing to thing to thing, free-associating its way through life. Each thing attention lands on triggers that chain of events the Buddha described: a sensation, a thought that goes with it, emotions that go with that, meaning that goes with emotion, and behavior that follows. You are walking along a path and you see a flower, which reminds you of the time you were in Hawaii at so-and-so's wedding, and the next thing you know you are caught up in, "Wasn't it tragic that that marriage didn't work out? Those poor children . . . I wonder if my children . . . ." You went from just walking along the path to feeling anxious, with no idea how that happened.

In sitting meditation, we practice withdrawing the attention from free-association and other forms of unconscious abandonment of ourselves to conditioned patterns. We bring the attention back and let it reside in awareness. It goes off again, because that is its habit, and we bring it back. It sits here for a while, with the breath, with awareness. It takes off again. We pull it back. It takes off. We pull it back.

When we get up from the cushion and shift into walking meditation or working meditation or whatever, we practice the same thing. We notice where the attention goes, and we bring it back to the breath. It goes off, we bring it back. Pretty soon those habits of attention are being changed. The attention now develops a tendency to be present. It will actually come back to the breath without being called. We may suddenly realize that nothing is going on with us, we are just walking along breathing, and attention is right here with us.

As that change happens, people say things like, "I feel better. I don't know why, but when I meditate, my life gets better. It makes no sense to me, but it happens." Attention is no longer racing around and dragging us into trouble—trouble that does not exist anywhere except in our illusory sense of ourselves as separate from all that is. Increasingly, attention simply rests in awareness of what exists here and now.

find out for yourself

When I talk about awareness I mean the whole field embraced in our consciousness. To me, it seems that attention moves around from one thing to another within the field of awareness.

Those terms are used in different ways, however. Some people talk about awareness the way I talk about attention, as if awareness moves around. But it is not my experience that awareness moves around. To me, it seems that awareness is; attention moves within it.

Where does attention come from? That is for you to find out. To me, it is not helpful to come up with pat answers to those extremely deep kinds of questions. It is better to pursue those experiences on your own and see for yourself.

Do not accept my perception that attention moves within the field of awareness. Is that so? What is your experience? You might use different words for it; you might talk about it in a completely different way. You find out for you.

the centered place

When we drop everything and come back to the breath, there are no problems, no questions, no conflicts. There is no difficulty with anyone or anything.

The moment we move away from simply being present to what exists in the moment, all of the problems of the world come into being. When we turn our attention back to the present moment, the problems vanish. War, torture, starvation, disease, children dying—in this place, in this moment, does all that exist? Who could prove it? There is no evidence of it. But as soon as we leave the present and get lost in the world of conditioning, of separateness, there it all is again.

People will assert that it is irresponsible to turn to that place of being centered, to take refuge in the present moment and not participate in the problems of life. But from that place, we do actively participate in life. We can see how people see things as problems, and we can see why. It is just that we do not see those things as problems.

We notice that every time we return to that centered place, there is that pervasive sense of well-being. Whatever is in that moment is met by that same well-being. Eventually, we realize that returning to that place actually produces the well-being, so it does not matter what the external circumstances are.

in agreement

In the beginning, turning away from conditioning and bringing the attention back to the breath can involve a laborious process of reminding yourself. You watch a criticism of yourself arise in your mind. You see that some part of you is measuring you all the time, comparing, keeping score, and you simply remind yourself that it is not necessary to do that.

It is also not necessary to defend yourself. It may be reassuring to tell yourself something like, "I'm just a person, and this is how people are."

"But you aren't as good as . . . ," your conditioning will put in.

"No, I'm not."

"And you're always forgetting . . . ."

"Yes, that is so."

"And you never have and never will . . . ."

"I agree. I'm that way, too, and that way, and that way, and all those ways. Yes. I accept it all."

Nothing defuses egocentricity quicker than agreeing with it.

what keeps us from spiritual practice?

Meditation is like eating right and exercising in that you do not have to enjoy it for it to have an effect. If you practice lifting weights, your muscles will get stronger regardless of how your mind felt about it while you were doing it. Sitting in meditation is helpful even when we are tired or anxious or there is something else to do that seems more important. Different parts of us will have their own experiences of it, including hating it and wanting to be anywhere else, but the power of the sitting is still there. We do not have to have a "good" meditation. It does not have to produce any insight or awareness. We can sit there and fidget and be miserable, and it still works. We are being transformed by the experience.

I know I feel better when I eat right and exercise and meditate; I know I am happier. So what is the point of not wanting to do them? It can be very interesting to figure out what part of me does not want to do something I know to be helpful.

If sitting meditation seems boring, and we believe that is what keeps us from doing our spiritual practice, we may want to challenge that idea and just keep sitting. How long will we have to sit with the boredom? Until we realize that we are not going to quit because of it. Until we say, "Okay, I'll just sit bored."

The boredom will turn into terror when we begin to challenge our conditioning, when we question its authority to tell us what our experience is. As long as we are thinking, "Sitting is boring, and there is so much else to do, and I'd rather do those things," our conditioning is dictating our experience. But we could say, "Well, sitting may be boring, but I'm going to sit anyway. For the next six months, I'm going to sit every day." We still believe there are all those other things to do, things that need to be done and need to be done now. But once we refuse to go along with those conditioned ideas, our relationship with our conditioning is changed.

Then watch the conditioning escalate. As long as we are willing to believe that the voices of conditioning are "me," that "I" am making the decisions, they can be fairly benign. But the moment we say, "This time there's going to be a different decision," it is a huge threat to ego.

In the world of egocentricity, meditation is something you should do because you want to be a spiritual person. It is hard, and you have to talk yourself into it. In the world of freedom from egocentricity, meditation makes life worth living. Once you cross that line, there is no problem.

The way you get to that line is to watch closely and figure out everything egocentricity does to keep you from getting to that line. With each new difficulty, a conditioned reaction stops you, but you begin to see how it stops you. It stops you again, and you see through that. Pretty soon, there is nothing stopping you. You just hop over the line, and there you are.

It is not that we have to first find the willingness and then sit down to meditate. It is that we have to turn away from the structures of resistance in order to allow the willingness to be there. Somebody told me when she becomes aware that she is angling for excuses to get straight to work in the morning and skip sitting, she allows herself to head for her desk, but she lets her left hand reach out and grab her cushion as she passes it. Then she puts the cushion on the floor, and once it is on the floor, it is much easier to actually sit on it.

If we wait for ourselves to become willing or try to make ourselves be willing to set aside the time and take the cushion down and put it on the floor and actually sit on it, there are too many ambush spots. Instead, we can let the moment of resistance be the signal to let go, to make a little space for that deeper part of ourselves.

the person who sits at six

It may seem as if we have moments of being present and that those are like grace or luck, in that we are not in control of when they happen. But it is very good to take charge of our luck, to give grace a chance.

We know that there are ways to increase our chances at grace. Silence, solitude, meditation, a regular time every day to come back to ourselves are ways of making ourselves available.

Is grace going to be there? Maybe not, but at least we are there, ready, in case it is. If any grace is going around, we will be open to it.

Let's say there is some aspect of being on retreat that you find helpful, something that helps bring your attention back to the moment, and you decide to introduce that into your regular life in some way. Maybe it is that on weekdays, you will do twenty minutes of sitting meditation at six o'clock.

A commitment like that serves as an external guide, just as the schedule does on a retreat: no matter how wacko you get, if you can follow the schedule, just putting the one foot in front of the other, you will survive. The difference is that at your house no one will write a little note, "You were not at meditation this afternoon." You will need to provide that guidance for yourself. It is a challenge, because something like this offers fertile ground for self-criticism.

Now, in setting up your own schedule, start small. Decide on something you feel you can commit to on a regular basis. Then—watch how your conditioning talks you out of it.

When you fail to live up to your commitment, the voices will start in. "You've never stuck to anything." But remember: beating yourself is not to be confused with spiritual practice. Just notice what the voices say. You can even take notes. If it is coming too fast, say, "Wait a minute, I'm trying to get this down. 'You've never stuck to anything.' All right, got that one. Go on." Or talk into a tape recorder. "'You don't have what it takes. You never have. Why fool yourself?'" Eventually you will have heard it all.

The next day is a new day, and you make your commitment again. If you keep it, great. If you don't, the voices come after you. You have already been through it, so you recognize what is happening. "Okay, I hear that. In fact, I've heard all of this before. Yes, it's sounding familiar." As you observe that self-hating process, it becomes less believable.

Eventually, you know yourself as a person who sits every weekday at six o'clock. That is who you really are, so that is what you are going to do. At a quarter to six, all sorts of excuses may arise. "If you can't keep your commitment every day, why bother? Meditation doesn't seem to be working, anyway." But it is a weekday, and it is getting toward six, and now is your time to sit. And you head for the cushion.

Making that commitment is the ultimate way of honoring yourself. Everything other than that is beside the point. It is a private experience between you and your heart. It is a very intimate relationship you are working on.

room on the cushion

Sitting in meditation opens our hearts. What wants to sit? Who we really are. What wants to be still? Stillness. The quiet, the peace, the well-being wants to be with itself, wants to experience itself. So when we sit, even if it is a fidgeting, wiggling, hate-every-moment-of-it-sit, what is sitting is that deepest part of us.

Continuing to sit reinforces that part of us who wants to sit. It also reveals the nature of the ego onslaught. Seeing that, our hearts open a little bit, and as our hearts open, there is more kindness. There is more ability to be present, to be open to and aware of something other than the conditioned structure that is maintaining itself against the inherent goodness of life.

It can certainly seem as if that person who wants to sit disappears as soon as we hit the cushion. We are bombarded with everything in the world, all our conditioned patterns, all our resistance, all our suffering. But that is all right, because there is room on that cushion for all of that to be there, along with who we really are.

the habit of nonreaction

It is hard to go up against egocentric conditioning because it seems as if conditioning has the power to wear us down, to out-last us. We might as well quit struggling, we think, because sooner or later we will give in to it.

In fact, if we sit still long enough, conditioning will wear itself out. We can begin by sitting still with something that is making us miserable. We just do not respond to that pull to get involved with it.

The attitude we bring to that is analogous to the kind of non-violent protest practiced by some of my personal heroes. It does not involve putting energy out and giving somebody something to resist, but being there, sitting down, staying still, and not moving. If somebody moves you, as soon as you get free from them, you come back and do the same thing over again. You keep doing that until you win. Whenever it has been done in that way, there has always been winning at the end of it.

That does not mean human nature will change, and it does not mean conditioning will change. We can offer our passive resistance, and conditioning may give up temporarily, but it will be circling around and coming in another door. However, as we get the hang of sitting still and not reacting, not giving our energy to condi-tioning, then it becomes less of a problem.

That is why we practice sitting in meditation when nothing is happening; it is much easier than sitting still in the middle of intense suffering. Even when nothing is happening, there is plenty to practice with. If I sit long enough, something starts to hurt. Okay, it hurts. I probably will not die of it. Now I am having a strong emotional reaction about it. Okay. I sit there with it, and pretty soon it goes away. Then something itches. Okay.

We develop a habit of sitting still as things arise and play themselves out for whatever period of time, and then they go away. The only way they can continue is if we engage with them, in which case we can make them last a really long time.

In this process, we become acquainted with whatever it is in ourselves that is unaffected by circumstances—because it is not separate from circumstances.

refuge in the breath

The breath is a refuge that is always there for us. Bringing our attention back to the present moment, to the breath, is like "king's X" in playing tag, a safe place where nobody can get you. We have to be pulled out of the moment for anything to happen to us. Anything and everything can pull us out of it—and we collude, we agree, we go along, back to the land of egocentric conditioning where suffering happens. But in any moment, we can go home to the breath.

I like "king's X" because you can call it and be safe anywhere you are, rather than having to get to some special place. Believing that we have to get to somewhere special in order to be free sets us up for suffering. But we can realize that wherever we are, we can come back to the breath, come back to the moment. It does not matter where we just were, it does not matter how bad it was. We just drop all that and come back to the breath. We can watch ourselves be pulled away, watch all the things we are suckers for, all the things we are willing to go along with. When we notice we are out there in our conditioning, instead of deciding we have done something wrong and beating ourselves up, we just come right back to the breath—and we are home free.

🪷 4 intelligence at work 🪷

The Buddhist path is based not on beliefs but on direct investigation of experience. The term dharma, in fact, means truth or law, in the sense of natural law; it means how things are. Meditation develops awareness and understanding of how things are.

In that process, we uncover dimensions of intelligence that most of us have scarcely imagined, far exceeding the common idea of intelligence as reasoning ability. Intelligence is, in this broader sense, the very substance of dharma practice. When we notice how much better our lives become when we meditate regularly, we are seeing the results of intelligence at work.

where joy comes in, and where it exits

A line in the Daily Recollection that is recited each morning at our monastery says that dharma is the "joy of intelligence knowing itself." Someone asked, "Where does joy enter into all this?"

I would suggest that it is more a question of where joy exits—or, more precisely, where we elbow it out. The joy is always there, but without consciousness, how can there be awareness of it?

My point is this: we waste a lot of time in which we could be experiencing the delights of life because we have been convinced that egocentricity is preferable to the joy of intelligence knowing itself. We would rather focus on what will happen later, how hard things are, how we would rather be doing something else, and so on. In giving our minds over to that kind of thing, we reduce the vast expansiveness of existence down to our petty concerns. Everything is available to us, and we manage to avoid it by choosing our little world of separateness and suffering. (I hope that does not sound as if I am putting people down, because of course the only way I would know it is through personal experience.)

Many of us live with one foot in each world. We know the more expansive world exists; we have touched it many times. We know it is available to us, and yet—the small world of suffering is so familiar, so real, so *me*. Letting it go and putting both feet in the expansive world is a scary proposition.

The biggest stumbling block for most of us is that we have a simple misconception about life, in that we limit our idea of intelligence to what we can talk to ourselves about. The conditioned mind, focused on concerns about what has already happened and what is going to happen later and liking this thing and not liking that thing, is contained within a much more expansive intelligence that is not limited to human brain function.

In a way that is very difficult for us to imagine, intelligence just *is*. There is nothing outside it. Intelligence is that which animates all that is. If we attempt to reduce that to a concept that our conditioned mind can hold on to, it is like the toaster thinking that without it, electricity could not exist.

creating suffering

We can use anything at all to suffer over. For example, if I am building a house and I manage to make it beautiful, my conditioning may be to feel that if I can make it that beautiful, I should be able to make it twice as beautiful. Suddenly, I am no longer content to simply do the best I can. I am going to raise the standards until I am dissatisfied.

In somebody else's life, it can be obvious that suffering is being manufactured unnecessarily. Let's say you have a friend who is a therapist, and he is upset because insurance pays for a particular client to have only six weeks of therapy when six months is needed and ideally it would be six years. Your friend is treating this as both a personal attack by the insurance industry and proof of the collapse of the social order. From your point of view, it seems as if the client has already been helped, but your friend is clinging to these five or six personality quirks in his client that he still wants to work on. His attitude is that if only the insurance company would cooperate so there would be more time and money, he could turn his client into an ideal human being.

You think, "Come on, haven't you done what's important? Hey, let it go! I mean, insurance is nothing compared to the costs in building my beautiful home. I'm up against limits everywhere I turn. Let's face it, therapy can be a pretty vague area. A person may get better over the long run or may not; it's hard to tell. But

I'm talking *kitchens*—tangible stuff. Formica is something you can *touch*. And it's a choice I'll have to live with *every day*, morning, noon, and night. This is *real*."

Wanting things to be different, believing things should be different, and taking it all so seriously is a process of suffering that goes on within us, usually unnoticed. In that process we are pulled away from the present moment where there is nothing wrong and plunged into frustration and resentment and despair.

But we can see through that process. That is what we are looking for: when have we slipped over into something that makes us miserable? We cross over into suffering when we get caught up in the content of the situation.

Instead of doing that, we can look below the surface into the large picture. What do we really want? We want to contribute something to the world, whether it is through building a beautiful house or through working with people in therapy. And what are we actually contributing, by setting up standards that we cannot meet? We are simply creating suffering.

One of my favorite lines of spiritual wisdom is, "If you want an answer to the question *why*, look at the results." What is being created by what we are doing? Often, the answer is misery. The Buddha saw that this is so. He figured out how it works. And he offered us a different way of approaching life.

mystery story

I like to compare spiritual practice to mystery novels. I have a friend who, knowing a number of religious people, has concluded that all religious people love to read mysteries. I do not know if that is true, but I think it is an interesting idea, because there is a certain parallel between the two.

Let's say you encounter a mystery: you just found a dead body outside the meditation hall. It is up to you to figure out what happened. Where are you going to start in solving this case? Maybe you start by thinking you have got to know who committed the murder. Already you are expecting yourself to understand what happened and how it happened and who did it, and you have not yet even looked at the body. Unless there are signs of foul play, how would you know that it is a case of murder?

Maybe it would be best to just sit down next to the body and wait for somebody wiser to come by and tell you what happened. Wouldn't it be lovely if Sherlock Holmes strolled out of the meditation hall and took over the case? If that is the way you respond to the situation, you can just notice that, and then you will have learned something about yourself.

To me, spiritual practice is like a mystery story in that we stumble onto something we have never encountered before. The intelligent approach is more like, "Wow, what have we here? Let me take a closer look. Now, how could this body have ended up in this position? What could have made this hole in the person's jacket? I didn't hear anything. Maybe I should glance around this whole area."

But enough of dead bodies: let's imagine that the object of your investigation is judgment, the judgment that goes on in you. Not that you would be judging judgment, but just examining it. What is judgment? Where does it come from? What does it do? When it is there, what is life like? When it is not there, what is life like? What parts of you judge? Are there good judgments? Bad judgments? Judgment is not something you need to hide or avoid or dispose of. It is like the body you found outside the meditation hall, a mystery you want to find out about.

If you look deeply and honestly, you may discover within yourself a belief that judgment is what makes you a good person. That could be scary to consider—that without judgment you might be "bad"—so you might be prepared for some resistance to the very thought of questioning judgment.

But here is the good news: while you are doing all this questioning and examining, you can go right on judging, just as you always have. It will not work to try to be different, because what you are trying to find out about is the way you *are,* the way you operate, the patterns in you. Be just the way you have always been, with this difference: do not believe any of it, and pay close attention to all of it.

As with Eastern religions in general, Buddhism offers great spaciousness. In pursuing whatever mystery we are on to, there is no rush. There is no Judgment Day around the corner; that body is not going anywhere. So, after some period of time during which you apply yourself diligently to observing your own judgment, you will reach a point of knowing all there is to know about it. It does not mean you will not continue to judge—just like solving a crime does not bring a dead body back to life—but you have the satisfaction of being able to say, "Okay, that mystery is solved."

observing obsession

If we are paying attention, we may notice that our first response in certain situations is to start obsessing. That is good to know. "When a certain thing happens, my first reaction is to think about it obsessively." We also can become aware that no matter what it is that we obsess about, it follows the same pattern.

The internal process of obsessing has happened through our lives with a variety of subjects. We are just going along, and, whoosh—all of a sudden we are obsessing about something. We believe it completely, it is terribly dramatic, and everything else falls into the background.

Isn't that curious? What would it be like to really pay attention to obsessing, to put it under close observation?

Here it comes again. This time we may notice physical sensations. "Wow, my heart starts doing this, and my stomach starts doing that." Then those sensations are gone; it all passes through and is over with. How does it start up again? In asking that kind of question, we focus not on the particular content but on the process.

Instead of instantly reacting to an incident—say, something that has hurt us—if we play the whole pattern of obsession one more time, bringing that experience in and sitting still with it and just observing it, then we may hear from different parts of ourselves: the parts who want to blame, the parts whose feelings are hurt, the parts who are frightened, the parts who do not want to lose a friend, the parts who want to review all similar incidents from the past. To have all that information could be quite illuminating. And how different to go into it feeling that we need to be with the experience and understand it, to stay with it until we move through it or see through it, instead of using the experience to perpetuate our suffering.

The next time a situation arises that provokes obsession, we can remember what we know about it. "Obsession: that's exactly what I'm doing, and I know how it's going to be." After we have observed that process many times, we may even have a sense of how long we are likely to obsess. It can be over with in as little as twelve hours, but at times we have pushed it close to a week. So the range is somewhere in between half a day and six or seven days, and then it will be all over.

Then we will—do what?

Again, we notice: what do we do when we finish obsessing? Well, then we seem to move into distraction. Two days ago we could not think about anything but what we were obsessed about, and now we are busy, busy, busy with something else. After we have watched that for a while, then the next thing will happen, and the next thing will happen. And we will recognize it as a *process*.

To me, the process is ever so much more interesting than the conclusion. The process is participatory, it is life living. The more we observe the process, the less power it has to run our lives. The way to diminish its power is simply to sit still with it and watch, watch, watch.

the knotted scarf

The Buddha talked about an individual life being like a long silk scarf with a series of knots tied in it. The knots represent our conditioned patterns, the ways in which we cause ourselves to suffer. We come to spiritual practice when our scarves are so knotted that there is no room for another knot. Spiritual practice is untying those knots.

As you start your practice, the first knot you encounter is the one that was most recently tied. It is not easy, but if you keep working at it, eventually you can untie that knot. Then, of course (I don't know what you were expecting) there is another one. The second one is a little tougher, but you work and work and work, and you make your way through it.

So, going back through this single lifetime of knots, there is the one from just yesterday, and there are ones that were tied when you were ten and four and three years old. It is important to remember that you do not want to let the three-year-old in you be trying to untie knots; that is a job for someone with experience. Any three-year-old confronted with needing to untie a hard knot is, quite naturally, going to feel inadequate.

As you go along, it is true that the knots become harder to untie, but it is also true that you get better at untying them. And the knots are not all that different from one another; it isn't as if you will suddenly come across a knot that is unlike any other in the history of knots. They seem different when you first encounter them, but soon you recognize that they are all pretty much the same. As you work with each new knot, in the way that you are learning in dharma practice, it begins to loosen and finally it releases. And there you have it—another success.

The experience you gain each time you untie a knot gives you the encouragement you need to take on the next one. After a while, you approach the whole process with confidence and lightness and, increasingly, gratitude.

ego up against the wall

If I walk into the kitchen and smell gas, I know what that smell means, and I know what can happen if that smell is not attended to. Before I knew what that smell was, I could have gone to bed one night and not gotten up in the morning. In the same way, it is important to know the signs and potentials and movements of egocentricity, to recognize them for what they are, and to take steps to deal with them. If I smell gas in the kitchen, I open the doors and windows, find the leak, get it fixed. Within ourselves, similarly, there are steps we can take to protect ourselves from the suffering caused by egocentric conditioning.

Let's examine one conditioned process, guilt. Guilt is a process that does not require specific content. As long as you maintain the internal process of feeling guilty, guilt will always be there about something. But awareness of that process can stop it.

You can be just going along, and a voice in you says, "You're lazy." When you hear that message, you feel guilty, just like Pavlov's dogs salivating when a bell rings. That is conditioning. The two events have nothing to do with each other, but, quite predictably and automatically, hearing "You're lazy" produces a feeling of guilt.

How could you break that pattern? You might notice exactly what happened and write it down on a little note and stick the note on the wall. "The voice says 'You're lazy,' and then I feel guilty." It could be a cartoon: "You're lazy" is in a balloon above the head of the person. Next panel: person feels guilty. There you have the conditioned pattern of response. From now on, when you hear that message inside your head, you know what the result will be. It is like knowing what it means when you smell gas.

"When that happens, this is how I feel" applies to all sorts of conditioned reactions. It takes so long to work through even one of those patterns because ego is very resistant. We try to deny what our conditioning does to us; we hide out, hoping it will forget about us. But go right on in there. "A voice says I'm lazy, then I feel guilty." There it is. You diagram it and put it on the wall, and you check in with it every day. You actively listen for that voice.

Pretty soon you will hear another voice, presenting the other side of the issue. "But you are too tired to work hard." Then watch what happens: you believe you are too tired, and you feel inadequate, overwhelmed, depressed. Lay all that out. "The voice says this, I feel that." What happens to you emotionally? What happens to you physically? What happens to you mentally? Chart the whole thing. Pretty soon you will have seen everything there is to see about that particular piece of your conditioning.

An essential ingredient in this is a sense of adventure and fun. If it is as grim as life and death, you have lost before you started. It has to have that light tone to it. On the one hand, it is serious business, because what motivates us is being sick of having our experience controlled by forces we do not understand. But our approach to that is more in the spirit of play: we are going to put on our boots and our six-shooters and head down Main Street, and we are going to confront those culprits. And from now on, we are going to have a different relationship.

Once you have seen everything there is to see about guilt, you can tackle another conditioned pattern. Next! You take on the next piece, and then the next. There is a tremendous sense of well-being that comes with that. You are no longer ducking and hiding through your life. Everything is right out there, and you are actively dealing with it head-on.

It can sound laborious to have to do this with every one of those patterns in our lives. I assure you, though, it is no more laborious than living with them.

As with the Buddha's image of the knots in the scarf, you untie each knot of conditioning, one at a time, until they are all gone. Nothing is left unfinished, nothing is left undone. Then you can lay the scarf out on the ironing board and press it out so smoothly that there is not a wrinkle left.

no self

One of my favorite books is *Ask the Awakened* by Wei Wu Wei, and my favorite line from it is something like this: "Why do we suffer? Because ninety-nine and forty-four one-hundredths percent of what we do is for the self. And there isn't one." I remember reading along about four pages into that book and feeling my mind begin to scrunch down and twist and contort. I knew that reaction meant that the information was penetrating, so I went ahead and read it just to take it in, but with no illusion of comprehending what I was reading.

What we can and cannot know is very interesting and extremely subtle. We have to agree that our words miss the point entirely, that this subject simply cannot be talked about in a direct way. Once we agree to that, we can go ahead and talk about it.

That which is essential cannot be grasped, because it requires someone separate from it in order to grasp it. Just saying that, we can see that that which is separate from it could never grasp it; the very separation precludes that. But the separation creates an illusion of being able to grasp something.

Does that mean that all we will ever be able to grasp is the illusion of separateness? No. That idea presupposes that that which is essential is not inherently intelligent, that "knowing" requires a subject and an object. That presupposition is so deep because we see ourselves as subject with everything else as object;

even when we are seeing ourselves as object, we take the position of identification with subject.

If we consider that that which cannot be grasped is intelligence itself, can that intelligence, without subject or object, experience? I would suggest that nothing else ever happens. The idea that there is something separate from that experience of intelligence itself—that is the illusion.

a heavy mist

The first time I really saw how projection works, my whole world shifted to accommodate the understanding that things are the way they are because I am the way I am. Since then, I have had the same insight countless times, each time at a deeper level: oh—*that, too!* It seems as if the scope of what is projected is increasing, but it is just that my understanding is expanding to grasp larger and larger implications of it.

When I first read *Zen Flesh, Zen Bones* about thirty years ago, I had no idea what those stories were all about. Six months later, after I had begun to meditate, I looked at it again, and my reaction was, "Oh, I see what this is referring to." A year later: "Okay. Yes." Two years later: "I get that. I know what that means." Five years later, I could actually explain my understanding of it.

So, we may not understand spiritual practice, but we pursue it anyway. In fifteen years, in twenty years, in twenty-five years, we will look back and see that our sense of what we are embarked upon has expanded and clarified.

This practice is like walking in a heavy mist. It penetrates slowly, permeating every, every, everything, until it reaches the bone and then inside the marrow of the bone. All along the way, we have had glorious moments of, "Yes, I get it! I see—yes, *yes!*" And then we walk on, into the mist ahead.

🪷 5 life expectancy 🪷

Our ability to imagine things we do not have, and the dissatisfaction that results, is a more or less constant feature of human existence. For many people, the hollowness of success attained in the material realm—the ordinary world of impermanence, of separateness from all that is, of egocentric grasping—provides the initial motivation to pursue spiritual practice. The first step on the path is to recognize our situation. Only through seeing life as it is, accepting and embracing it in compassion, are we freed from suffering over it.

the problem with hope

There is a bumper sticker that says, "I feel so much better now that I've given up hope." People may put that on their cars as a joke, but from a Buddhist point of view, it can be taken seriously.

We have tried living our lives in the hope that being nice and polite and crossing our fingers will get us what we want—but it does not work. The idea that we are going to do something in order to be different assumes that we need something we do not have, so we are lost before we even begin.

At the monastery, it is so refreshing for someone to come to me and say, "I really screwed up. I did this and this and this. And here is what I've seen in that experience." I much prefer that to having to track them down and say, "By any chance, does someone here know how that burned-up truck got in the courtyard?" In this practice we are not trying to be right, we are trying to end suffering, and hoping for things to be different simply gets in the way of that process.

If we realize that what we are looking for is what is causing us to seek, then it is clear that what we are looking for is right here. What are we doing to keep ourselves from recognizing that? That is where to look, rather than trying to change ourselves.

Once we give up hope, we are living in the moment we are in. Hoping for something to be different takes us out of the only moment we have. It is sometimes said that in Buddhism there is no room for hope. Yes, letting go of the illusion and helplessness we call "hope" does feel better—so much better that we would never want to go back to that way of looking at things.

Faith, to me, means something different. My teacher often said that faith is not something unknown and hoped for; faith is a knowing based on experience. Trust also is different from hope. As my teacher put it, perfect trust is that life will be what it is and people will be who they are.

In retrospect, we can see how each event in our lives, no matter how painful or humiliating, was critical in getting us to where we are now. Once we realize that, no matter what happens, we are deeply grateful for it. Once we know that there is only going to be whatever is, then we know beyond a shadow of a doubt that we cannot possibly make a mistake. From that perspective, there is no place for hope.

beyond comfort

A common expectation about spiritual training is that it should be nice. Everyone should be pleasant and holy and levitate around, smiling and flapping their little wings, and no one should ever do reprehensible things. We like to be comfortable. We like to be mirrored in a way that makes us feel good. We like being around someone holy because then we feel holy ourselves, we think elevated thoughts, we feel inspired. But what could we possibly learn in that? If we really want to do spiritual training, we have to start where we are, which is not pure and saintly.

The next time you pick up something to read, don't choose something because you think you will like it, because it will make you feel better about yourself. Read something because it pushes your edges, because it sets you off, because it will take you beyond your current idea of who you are. Practice that instead of going out into the world and saying, "That's wrong, he's wrong, she's wrong, it shouldn't be that way. Now I'll go home and read some nice religious philosophy and feel better about the whole thing." Not it.

In recent times, there is hardly a religion that has not suffered terrible scandals involving a spiritual leader. When two well-known Zen centers went through their well-publicized difficulties, one type of reaction was, "Well, I've been duped. I've been taken advantage of. I'm really upset. Therefore spiritual practice must be a crock, and I'm out of here." No matter what did or did not happen, that reaction is unlikely to lead to learning anything since it serves as an excuse to abandon spiritual practice. A different type of reaction was, "I am so uncomfortable over this. I bet there is a lot to be learned here. I assumed this, I believed that—now I can see that I wasn't paying any attention at all to what was going on in myself. That's something I want to look at. I'm just going to stay with my discomfort and see what there is to see." This approach can result in our learning everything there is to learn from the situation, because we are willing to risk feeling uncomfortable in order to enlarge our understanding.

If we run at the first hint of discomfort, we cannot win. But if we acknowledge that the learning available to us is *within* us, and we are willing to be uncomfortable in that process, we cannot lose.

no regrets

On retreat, people often discover that even the most wonderful fantasy cannot compare with the direct experience of life as it is going on around us. It is impossible to convince anybody who has not had that experience that it is true, and people will argue with me about it. Am I saying you should not daydream, or that you should give up your creativity or your imagination? No. Until you have the experience of actually being present in life, fantasy may be the best thing you have going. I would never suggest that someone give up the one pleasurable activity that is available to them.

I would suggest, however, that there is pleasurable activity yet to be discovered, which is the joy of being fully present to the moment one is in. It does not matter where you are, and it does not have to be anything extraordinary. If you are actually present, it is blissful. If you are not, it does not matter how beautiful a place is. How many of you have gone to great expense to travel to an extraordinary place and been miserable, or been so distracted that you were not there at all in any meaningful sense?

I suspect that the regret we feel over not having fully experienced life fuels a great number of rebirths. We think if we had it to do over, we would be different, more present to everything. The quickest check on that is tomorrow: if we cannot be different tomorrow, we are not likely to be different in another life.

There can be immense suffering because we were here together and were not truly present to each other and our lives. We missed the moment, we were doing something else, we were fantasizing, we were irritated, we were waiting for something better—anything but what is right here and now.

My encouragement is not to look back on what has happened, not to have any regrets. Regret is from the world of conditioning. There is no place for regret in the larger, more expansive world. What happened happened. We start over in each moment, here and now.

learning opportunities

We tend to believe that having enough information will enable us to be in control. If we are in control and do all the right things and do not make any mistakes, we won't get into trouble, and life will be good and everything will go well.

Then somebody else screws up in a way that prevents us from getting the information we need, and all of a sudden we do not know the right thing to do, we are in danger of making a mistake, and we get angry at that person. It seems as if that person is threatening our very existence, but what is being threatened is the existence and well-being of our egocentric conditioning.

In spiritual practice, that is really important to know. Whenever we have a reaction like getting angry, we can look to see what is being triggered, what is being affected. We are doing spiritual practice in order to find those conditioned places of suffering inside ourselves, to recognize them for what they are and be free of them. So, it is a really good deal when somebody screws up. In fact, if everything worked as perfectly as we like to imagine it should, we would never learn anything about ourselves.

On the other hand, if it feels as if being in a particular job or relationship is not good for you, then don't be there. People will protest that there may be more for them to learn in that situation. My response is, then you will be in it again. It may take a while to find the same relationship with a different person, or the same boss and the same coworkers in different bodies and the same job in a different location and with a different description, but we do it all the time.

We can have faith that doing whatever we do and paying attention to it will always be our best opportunity to see how we cause ourselves to suffer. The point to keep in mind is that whatever we do and whatever other people do can help us learn about ourselves. Life is a series of learning opportunities, perfectly matched to what we need to find out.

the radical implications of nonseparateness

Once at the Zen Center we did a series of workshops on death and dying, and as part of it, people wrote out their memorial services. Everybody planned to die sometime after their hundredth birthday, and they all wanted me to conduct their memorial services. I said no, I was not interested; I would be around a hundred and thirty by then.

Not that long ago, life expectancy was about forty years. By that age, life had been lived; people had reached maturity and had their families, and then they died. What is life expectancy now? Something like seventy-eight for women and seventy-two for men? And we are thrilled when the men get another year—"Okay, guys, you can relax; your life expectancy has gone up to seventy-three"— as if we are all going to participate in that statistical reality. But if you have ever been close to anyone who dies at that age, it seems wrong. "He was *so young*, only seventy-two—the prime of life!" In our conditioned way of choosing beliefs over experience, every-body is supposed to be born in a particular condition, namely, healthy, then grow through certain stages and live until we are an age that is deemed appropriately old.

It would be good to examine how the things that are all right with us and not all right with us tend to be a little self-serving. It is all right that other people in the world die naturally, because death is natural and we want to support those people in living their natural lifestyle, while we will do whatever necessary to avoid having that natural experience ourselves. We can support other people's children going through all kinds of character-building experiences, but not ours. We can feel angry and bitter when we see people who have better health than we do or more money or whatever it is, and we feel that our lives are all wrong in comparison to theirs. We believe that it is wrong for us to have diseases, wrong for us to have disabilities. How far removed from life have we become that the very processes of life are seen as a mistake?

That is the point of spiritual breakdown. Our entire lives are devoted to the service of an illusion. We sacrifice everything on the altar of I/me/mine, and it does not give us what we hoped it would give us. It does not make us feel good. It does not take care of us. It does not meet our needs. If it did, we would be the happiest people in creation, and we can look around and see that we are not.

The point I want to make is that actually letting go of the beliefs that support the illusion of a separate self will have far-reaching implications. We see every day what the illusion of separateness creates all over the world. Let us acknowledge that we are participating in that, and if we choose to let that go, these are some of the questions we are going to run into. If I am not separate, then where is "mine?" How can there be a "mine" that is not "ours?"

to exit from shared illusion

To pursue spiritual awakening when someone close to you is threatened by it takes extreme courage. You will be making a lot of changes. What will that do to your relationships? Will the people in your life still care about you? Will you still care about them? How different can two people become and still share an illusion?

If you see that the illusion you share with the other person is at the core of the relationship, and you no longer believe in that illusion, you are aware that the relationship may wither and die. Do you really want to let it go? No, part of you certainly does not. But you can see that the natural progression of clinging together in the shared illusion is that you both go under, and there is no one to save either of you.

The hard, courageous choice is to take the necessary steps on your own spiritual path toward exiting from the land of suffering. Most people are not concerned about being in the land of suffering. Either they are not aware of it, or they are not looking for a way out. There is nothing you can do except to know that it is not helpful to stay there with them.

In fact, I would suggest that the greatest gift you can give someone you love is to find that exit yourself. You will need to go through it first to make sure it is the way to freedom you think it is. Go out there into freedom and get comfortable, then come back into the land of suffering. Revisit all those miserable parts of yourself; experience suffering a little more, to be perfectly clear about it. Then find the exit again, and spend some more time in freedom. Go back and forth until you know both sides very well. Then station yourself next to the exit. Sooner or later, people around you will figure out where they are living and start looking for a way out. If you are standing at the exit with great confidence, they will trust you when you say, "It's safe. I've been through there. You can go yourself and see. I'll stand right here and hold the door open. If it's not what you want, you can always come back here."

Here is an old story about that. Four men are traveling across the desert. They pass a crossroads, and soon they come to a high wall, going both ways as far as you can see. The first man scrambles up the wall, and when he gets to the top and looks over, he gasps in amazement and leaps down on the other side. The other three look at each other, and the second one goes up, gasps, and goes over. The two left behind look at each other, and up goes the third one, and the same thing happens. The fourth man thinks, "This has got to be good." He climbs up, and at the top he looks over and sees—paradise. It is more beautiful than anything he has ever seen or heard of, it is beyond anything he could have dreamed.

The fourth man is just about to follow the others and go over, when a different viewpoint occurs to him. He realizes that paradise will always be there, and he knows where it is, and he can come back any time he wants. So he takes one more look, then he climbs down the way he came and heads back to the crossroads, where he waits for travelers. When someone shows up, he tells them about the wall and what is on the other side, and he gives them directions on how to get there.

That fellow is a bodhisattva. That is what bodhisattvas do; they stick around to show others the way. It is not a requirement, but it is an option.

6 applied spiritual practice

As we move beyond the limitations of our conditioned minds, a natural clarity and insight emerge. In the light of that intuitive intelligence, what we had considered to be problems are seen merely as situations to which we bring our best intention and best effort. We are more aware of our actions, and so we have more opportunities to consciously apply spiritual teachings in our lives. At the same time, a spontaneous wisdom becomes available to us, and our actions are characterized by increasing ease and effectiveness.

saying no to suffering

If we watch closely, we see that suffering begins when we leave this moment and allow our minds to project out into the past or the future. We can watch ourselves start the slide into suffering as we begin to imagine dire happenings and sink into doubt and fear and hopelessness. Then we can bring ourselves back and just say no. Each time we are tricked again by egocentricity, we can see that the result is suffering.

In the refusal to indulge in what leads to suffering, there is nothing hard or harsh. On the contrary, it is the kindest, most compassionate approach to life.

Think about giving a child all the candy she wants, then watching her eat too much and get sick. She wants the candy, you can't say no, she gets sick. Watching that happen over and over, you build your strength to say no. As much as she wants it, as much as she cries and carries on and is unhappy, you know what is going to happen if you give in, and you are not willing to pay that price.

In the same way, we learn to keep our awareness here in this moment. Eventually it is completely clear to us that out there, in the world of egocentric conditioning, danger lurks, and the only safe place is right here in the present. Saying no to everything else—that is spiritual practice.

is that so?

The idea that things have a place where they start and a place where they stop, that they are here but not there, this but not that, is a very specific belief system from which we unconsciously operate. It is so deeply ingrained that it is almost impossible even to grasp the possibility that it might be a belief system. My hope is that as we pursue spiritual practice, we will see how such ideas constitute the foundation of our conditioned idea of reality, and we will call them into question.

Almost none of what we have been taught to believe is true. The very point from which we begin to explore is an assumption that is not so—something as simple and basic as I am a "me" who is going to explore, or "I" am going to look into that. When our primary premise is erroneous, we can set off in a completely erroneous direction and wander around lost for a long time. So it is good not to believe anything and to be open to everything. Even if we have explored some aspect of our experience again and again, even if we have examined it so thoroughly, so deeply, so completely and absolutely that we *really know what is so* about it, well—maybe, maybe not.

It is difficult, because for the very "I" who is attempting to find freedom, the only possibility is a lack of freedom. We assume that we are in bondage, and then we begin to try to free ourselves. But as long as we believe we are in bondage, we will never be free.

What if we are not in bondage? What if there is nothing wrong?

Our whole structure is based on the assumption that there is something wrong. "Of course there is something wrong," we think. "People are starving. People are killing each other. Horrible things are happening all over the world." But what if that is not "wrong?" What if that is just the way it is?

Now, notice what arises in reaction to that idea: the feeling that if we are not doing something about it, we are irresponsible.

A friend of mine has a T-shirt that says "How beautiful to do nothing and then rest afterwards." *How beautiful to do nothing.* That points at something really big, because the doing we are conditioned to believe in is in fact the road to suffering.

What reaction does that bring up? "But if I don't do anything, how would I pay the bills? What would happen to me?"

It is like the reaction to the conscientious objector: "What would happen to us if everyone felt the way you do?" Well, we would all be conscientious objectors. What would happen to us if everybody approached life in this open and nonpersonal and exploratory way we are talking about? Well, we would have completely different lives. But we want to stay in our current belief system, from which we can look out at something different from it and say, "That isn't possible."

No, it is not possible in this belief system—which is not the same as its not being possible. Would we be fed, would we have a roof over our heads if we were not obsessed with doing? We believe that to live, we must do something. But is that so?

noticing noodling

Somebody was telling me about how he had been observing his behavior while he eats. He noticed that sometimes he dawdles over his food and sometimes he races through a meal. He was comparing those experiences and ruminating about that. My response was to call attention to the ruminating, or noodling, as I call it. Of all the things we might notice we are doing— dawdling, racing, comparing, noodling—if we were to prioritize those as subjects to look into, noodling would be at the top of my list.

Noodling gets in the way of seeing what is going on. If we make a decision and then get caught up in our conditioned notions about what we should have done, it prevents our seeing what actually does happen. We decide we are going to change jobs, leave our relationship, buy a new car—whatever we decide— and the voices of egocentricity kick in with the same old back and forth: "This will work for me/this won't. This I like/this I don't." Good/bad, yes/no.

If we have been paying attention, we pretty much know what those voices are going to say on any subject—the standard list of dualities. An old Buddhist saying is, "When the opposites arise, the Buddha mind is lost." We usually see as much as we are going to see about a subject in the present moment; we are not going to gain much information by leaving this moment and going off into trains of conditioned dualistic thought.

When our attention is here in the present, the time will come to eat, and then we can be present as we eat. We can notice that sometimes we dawdle and sometimes we race. If we are ruminating, we will miss both of those experiences. Instead, we just *notice* what is going on when we are dawdling and what is going on when we are racing. What is the experience itself?

Then, we can notice the tendency to get caught up in ruminating about the experience, going back and forth about what it means, questioning whether what we are doing is actually dawdling or racing, along with making judgments about that. Most of the time, when we are caught up in it that way, we do not even notice when the dawdling or racing comes to an end. It could be helpful to take a larger step away from it and watch that back and forth as a process, to lose interest in dawdling versus racing and to simply watch how often we find ourselves caught up in the noodling.

At some point we realize that we could spend the rest of our lives lost in noodling over an endless variety of subjects—or, we could be here in the present moment.

decisions

For those of you who do not see the difference between noodling and awareness arising, I would encourage you to look for it, because I am strongly suggesting that there is a difference—and that difference is the source of suffering in life. Noodling maintains the illusion that there is someone outside of life that can decide the best way for life to go. And that is a pretty reliable guarantee of suffering. In the same way, the notion of an ideal decision brings with it the possibility of a less than ideal decision, which maintains the illusion of a parallel reality in which something different happens from what is actually happening.

It is helpful to me to realize that I do not make decisions; they just get made. For example, at meal time, it may occur to me that I could take this opportunity to eat more slowly. By the time I have that thought, the decision is already made. When I say the decision is already made, I may be using a different definition of "decision," because for me, deciding is not the noodling part. Deciding is what presents itself in life in that obvious kind of way: I have the thought, and it is decided.

What if you are trying to decide between two jobs? You have a job, but the possibility of a better job arises. There is a trade-off, however, because you will have to move, and it will cost more to live near the better job. You win a little, lose a little. That is where agony can really get a grip on you. (Can you imagine life handing you a much better job in a place that costs less and is in every way more desirable? We tend not to remember instances of that.) What actually has happened is that you wanted a better job, and one has appeared. I love that! How do we make it into a problem? By saying, "Yes, but it will be more expensive for me to live there."

Here is another situation. It's spring, you have a couple of hours, and you realize you could go to the nursery and pick out some plants for your garden. With the introduction of the topics of time and nursery, the relationship is already established, and the decision is made. It occurs to you that you want the plants, there is time to get them, and you proceed toward the nursery. It is the same as looking down at the fuel gauge in the car, seeing that the gas is low, looking up and seeing a gas station, and deciding to get gas. If there is nothing separate from that experience, then you pull into the gas station, and there is simply the one experience: need gas, gas station, pull in, fill up.

"Ah," someone will ask, "What if the decision is between going to the nursery and getting gas?" Well, you could simply get the plants and then get gas. But coming in behind that awareness is the conditioned voice that says, "But, you know, it might be more important to get gas first." Then we hear, "Yes, but don't forget that you need to . . . And what about this other thing? . . . Maybe you should . . . ." That is noodling, pure and simple. It is completely different from awareness arising in the moment.

Once the noodling starts, instead of simply needing to get plants and needing to get gas and doing the obvious things to meet those needs, you have a problem. It is presented so logically that you can go forever with it. Once you allow in, "Oh, that's true, I could do that other thing," then the next thing comes along, and the next thing, and the next thing, and pretty soon you have a review of all the things on your list that have been overlooked and should be done right away. Pretty soon that period of time you had is gone, and you will have spent it agonizing about all the things you have not done, and then you are exhausted and depressed.

The next question ups the ante: what if you run out of gas on the way to the nursery? Ah, that we call a spiritual opportunity; it is the essence of spiritual practice. We can deal with such situations in the present moment, or we can suffer over them.

Believing that noodling—our conditioned responses—will enable us to control life is signing a contract with the Devil. The second-guessing, the figuring it out, the trying to control, the egocentric scrambling for place—if we believe all that is going to get us what we want in life, the suffering that lies ahead will be great. The postmortem analysis can turn any life experience into misery.

When we are caught in our conditioning in one of those situations, trying to get out is like trying to get free from one of those traps the monkey puts its hand into to get a banana then can't pull its hand back out of. Trying to get back to center when we are stuck is just like that: the more we struggle, the worse it is. Better to just stop, right where we are, and ask, "Where am I?" And it is easy to see: "I'm stuck, ruminating over this decision." That is the perfect time to explore that experience of suffering. What does it feel like? What is involved? How does the world appear from that point of view? Before we know it, of course, we are back at center, because what we have done is disidentify from the ruminating in order to watch it, and now our relationship to it is totally different.

The secret of getting back to a centered place (rather than to a part of our personality who hates ruminating, for instance) is genuinely wanting to know about ruminating, as opposed to wanting to figure out the right decision. If we are ruminating and we feel helpless and hopeless, then we are trapped in a victimized relationship to ruminating, locked in a death dance with it. When we become *interested* in the ruminating, rather than in the content of any specific rumination, poof—we are free from it. And the decision will make itself.

certainty

I would hope that I never know for sure what is the right thing to do, because when we know what is right, we tend not to take the crucial step of turning back to ourselves, to look within, to listen for the still, small voice of the heart. Even if in some situations I felt completely convinced that a particular action was right, I would want a red flag to go up as a warning that I might not be clear and centered on the issue involved.

Only egocentricity is certain about what is right. Only egocentricity wants to make sure, to pin things down. Living from the heart, there are no guarantees, no certainty—only moment-to-moment freedom.

drama

When life is going well for us, there is an illusion of being in control. We think we must be doing something right, until at some point it is not working the way we want it to. We don't just say, "Well, it worked for a while," and forget about it; we feel we have to do something. And what do we do? Get upset. Gosh, that makes a big difference, doesn't it?

For egocentricity, the good times are not nearly as attractive as the times when there is a great deal of dissatisfaction and agitation. We can go along for a while with nothing much happening, but once ego slips out of center-stage position, we can just know that something will come along to get upset about. If there is nothing at hand to cause a problem, we can always dig around in the memory storage unit for past sins and crimes; any old thing will serve the purpose.

Sometimes people say that without the inner drama, our lives would be bland. That would be fine if we actually experienced it that way. But we have a low threshold for suffering. We can be having a good time up to a point, then all of a sudden we are not in charge of what is happening. It is no longer amusing or pleasant or exciting, and we do not like it at all.

If you think the dramas of egocentricity are necessary for life to be interesting, I would encourage you to spend an extended period of time without being dominated by your conditioning and then report back. I have never known anybody who had an experience of living without suffering who chose suffering because it is more interesting.

It is not easy to step out of that drama, but we can. We can simply say, "I don't think I'll participate in that. I think I'll just breathe. I'll just see what it feels like to be in this circumstance. I'll watch the sensations in my body, watch the connections to thought patterns, watch how emotions arise and pass away. This is a good opportunity to be quiet and still and observe all that." It's good to remember that we have to be outside life to feel upset by the way life is.

building trust

Parts of ourselves that need love and kindness and compassion are desperately trying to get our attention, but they have a hard time being noticed as long as we are busy giving our energy to ego-centricity. As we acknowledge those aspects of ourselves, as we extend compassion to what was previously judged unacceptable, we increase our ability to experience and identify with the compassionate nature that is our essence.

It is wonderful when we are able to comfort and heal the parts of us that are suffering. Far more important, though, is that the compassion expands to include more and more and more. It is like building a friendship. You get to know somebody, and you see a little bit of them. As you spend time together, trust builds, and they let you see a little more. If that goes well, and they feel accepted, they let you see more. With time, if the acceptance is consistent, then pretty soon the person feels comfortable being all of who they are with you.

That is what we are doing within ourselves. We are building that kind of loving, accepting, compassionate relationship with this one person whose suffering we have the ability to end, ourselves. And that is how we will end it: through that love and compassion. Not through assisting this person through a course of self-improvement to become someone different who can be accepted, but through accepting this person as is.

reassurances

In all the time I have been working with people, nothing I have done has stirred up so much resistance as the mere request to say something kind to yourself. "Well, *that's* not Zen." Immediately, people become experts on what Zen is and is not, and they are certain that saying something kind to yourself is not Zen. Now, if I encouraged them to say unkind things to themselves, they would accept it in a flash and believe they were doing deep spiritual practice.

What we call "reassurances" are words or phrases we say to ourselves as reminders of what we know is true about us. Reassurances simply state what is so, for example: "There is nothing wrong," or "I am fine the way I am," or "Life is manageable." Not swinging to the other end of the continuum: "I am the most gorgeous, brilliant, altogether fabulous individual ever to exist." (If you continue with this practice, you will discover that you are in fact all of those things, but for now, let's just go with what is obviously possible.) What we are used to, what feels right, is within the narrow range between "I am the worst person" at one extreme and "I'm really not too terribly bad" at the other, with occasional flashes of "I'm so much better than those other people." It is difficult to find the middle ground of being just fine.

Will saying reassurances produce an effect? And how! If they had no effect, egocentricity would be happy to have us mindlessly mumbling reassurances all day long. But ego is terrified of our bringing consciousness to a reassurance that states what we really are.

Repeating reassurances to yourself is beneficial in two ways. First, there will not be room enough for the negative messages to come in. Second, the consciously chosen reassurance about what is true for you will become your reality. In fact, it is your reality, and by saying it, you will simply become aware of it.

heads up

When you are caught in an aspect of conditioning that is misery-producing, one way to stay in it is never to look up. It does not matter where you are, inside or outside. But especially if it is a beautiful day, never, ever look up, because there could be a split second when you could be captivated by the beauty of nature and forget to be miserable.

That would bring you back to a larger perspective than the one ego wants you to stay stuck in. If you are looking down at the ground, nothing is stopping the brainwashing system of conditioning from constantly telling you who you are and what is wrong and what the world is like and how nothing is ever going to work.

Spiritual practice interferes with that process. It involves using everything we can get our hands on to interrupt that brainwashing mechanism and open ourselves to the joy of life.

like little children

One of the most important pieces of information for us on the spiritual path is that we must "become as little children." Most of us say, "Oh, yeah, I know that one," and dismiss it. But it is good to understand what that idea is all about.

In meditation we do not have to know anything; we do not have to be experts. Many people begin sitting meditation with ego trying to breathe for them, and they choke and sputter and cough and gasp and carry on, because ego cannot breathe. Being able to just sit there and watch the body breathe, rather than assuming there is a right way to breathe, is a huge step in practice. In fact, we do not know how to breathe. We cannot make breathing happen. We do it without knowing how, the way young children do everything.

I am not talking about a young child as viewed by an adult but a young child's view of the world. The child does not assume, does not live in the future, does not cling to the past. The child has no illusion of control, no investment in an identity. The child embodies present-moment awareness, completely alive and open to whatever is going on.

Because we have very little experience of someone who has that simple, innocent, present attitude of mind, we assume that such a person might be incapable of operating in a functional way in the world. But there is nothing about that attitude that would keep us from going to work, paying the bills, being productive and responsible. There is nothing about that innocence and spontaneity and enthusiasm and fascination with life that would keep us from being successful.

facing difficulties

We can come up against some difficulty on a retreat and tell ourselves that we do not want to face it right now, so we will wait until we get home. We do not ask ourselves how it would make it better to wait. We just say we will deal with it later, then that idea sort of trails off into nothingness. The picture fades, the music comes up, and that is the end of it.

Some people who started out with me years ago then disappeared are coming back now. When they started spiritual practice, it seemed like a drag. It is true that meditation is demanding. It is uncomfortable. It causes you to look at stuff you do not want to look at. If you stay with spiritual practice, you might give up habits that you do not want to give up. Not that anybody says you have to, but you know that if you keep paying attention, it is going to come to that. So some people drift off to live their idea of the good life.

It saddens me when people drift away from spiritual practice. Once they have worked with me, I love them, and it is sad to see people you love wander away into what you can be pretty sure is an increasingly unhappy future. It has never been my experience that ignorance and delusion improve anything, and I know that is the choice they are making. People return to spiritual practice when they have reached a point in their lives when escape is no longer possible.

To anyone who has not reached that stage, I offer this: avoiding and postponing is not a good approach. Now is the time to face it. When something comes up that is hard and scary, just remember that putting it off is not going to improve the situation.

Running is the worst strategy. People who know about these things say that if you come across a wildcat in the woods, never turn your back on it. Even if it seems that running is your best option, don't do it. Stand still and make yourself as big and as loud as you possibly can.

That is a good strategy in coming up against your own egocentric conditioning. With facing ego, though, I would add one piece of advice: run right at it. There is nothing to be gained by waiting.

7 the often-neglected yet 🪷 all-important third noble truth 🪷

The third of the Four Noble Truths proclaimed by the Buddha after his enlightenment is that freedom from suffering is possible. Easy for him to say, we think; when it comes to our own lives, we are not so sure. Why not? Perhaps the answer to that question is all that stands between us and the liberation we long for.

peace of mind on a sinking ship

There is a way in which it is true that life is not always wonderful and perfect. But there is another way in which life *is* wonderful and perfect. The difference is in how we live it.

Whatever we are experiencing at any moment does not have to be resisted or improved or analyzed. It is possible simply to open oneself to whatever is here. If we are not as happy as we would like to be, we simply notice that. Then we have a chance to find out what it is like for a human being to have that experience. That is very different from assuming that something is wrong.

If we are experiencing a glad well-being for anything that is, just because it is, if we are simply happy to be alive, happy to be human, then we are just as happy to be unhappy as we are to be happy, because all of it is being alive. When we are fully aware and living the experience, it is not unhappiness any more. It is more a fullness, a really being.

One Zen master compared life to walking down to the end of the dock, getting into a boat, sailing out, and sinking. Yes, that is what it is like. It is not as if the boat will sail into the sunset forever. It will sink, and our lives will be finished. A big catastrophe.

And yet, within that picture, we do not want to forget the Third Noble Truth: there is an end to suffering. This is Buddhism, after all.

not to insult god

Spiritual practice offers really wonderful things, but you have to be willing to receive them. If someone offers you something wonderful, and your response is rejection—even if it takes the form of "No, thanks, really," with an illusion of humility in that—it would be good to look a little closer. There could well be a whole lot of ego lurking right behind that refusal, saying ardently, *no, no, no.* Accepting the goodness of life is very threatening to egocentricity.

Our world, *this* world, *is* the Garden of Eden. But some people believe that if they do not approve of everybody and everything in the Garden, they need to do something about it, and what they do is almost always destructive and punitive. That is egocentricity at work.

People will say that it is not possible to end suffering in this lifetime; we may talk about it, but it is not really possible. Yes, it is possible. And to uncover a belief that says it is not possible is quite helpful. What is it in you that says, "I can't want that. That's too big. That's too much. That's too good"?

Yes, you can awaken. I would go so far as to say you should. I say that in the same sense that, in the Jewish tradition, it is considered an insult to God not to enjoy what you have been given.

Those of us who have the awareness, the sensitivity, the great privilege—all the things necessary to awaken and to end suffering in this lifetime—need to take that opportunity very, very seriously. As the Buddha pointed out, we never know when such an opportunity will arise again.

open and closed

We talk about the heart opening and closing. There are physical sensations that suggest that the center of our being actually opens and closes, depending on life circumstances. But couldn't it be that the heart is always open, and when we are identified with conditioning, we close down around it?

When life hits us with such serious situations—problems with health, work, relationships, say—that we are suddenly (if briefly) jolted out of our ability to maintain the structures of egocentricity, it seems as if the heart is open. It is as if ego is too stunned to stay in charge, and it just says, "Here, heart, you take over. I'm outta here. You're on." We could conclude that either the process of stunning the ego causes the heart to open or (my suspicion) the heart is always open, just waiting for the conditioning to fall away and reveal it.

It is not that, as conditioning would have us believe, we need to change ourselves or fix ourselves or improve ourselves so that we can have an experience of bliss, and then the bliss will grow through some effort on our part. What I experience, and what I hear that other people experience, is that bliss is here when we stop doing everything else. We can be thoroughly distracted, totally involved in maintaining the structures of ego, but when attention and awareness come back to the present moment, bliss is what is here. It seems as if the energy can be in either place—out there maintaining egocentric structures or simply residing in what is right here when we are not doing all that.

Can we choose to be with our hearts in this moment? Can we bring into our hearts whatever arises in this moment? Even if it feels as if our hearts are closed, can we expand our compassion to include that, too?

staying put

There are two fundamental approaches to addressing something that seems like a problem. One is letting our attention be drawn out away from us to focus on the problem externally. The other is bringing that problem into us, into the present moment, into the heart, and dealing with it here. Discerning the difference between those approaches is an important skill we develop in spiritual practice.

I have an image of a medical clinic where the doctor gets called out to one thing after another. Anyone who comes to the clinic finds nobody home, because the person in charge is busy running around somewhere else. People are dying on the doorstep.

That is how it is within us. Most of the time, we are off somewhere else. Do you ever think how self-indulgent it is to maintain ego all day? We have to think about this, then we have to think about that. We worry about these things, and don't forget those. Make that list, make that decision. It is a full-time occupation.

To the degree that we can let go of the ego maintenance efforts, we can turn to the second approach: accepting responsibility for staying put and letting it all happen within us. It is a big savings of time and energy; it is very efficient to live in the present. We can learn to focus our attention here and require anything that wants assistance to come to us in this place of stillness and well-being.

The body has concerns? Fine, this is a good place for them to come to. There are concerns about job and money and future? Fine, those concerns can come here. Everything is welcome to come in and be cared for here, but we are not leaving here to go out there and worry about it.

catching a glimpse of awareness

One of my favorite quotations of all time is from Meister Eckhart: "The eyes with which I see God, God sees me." And one of my favorite parts of this practice is how we can use projection to see ourselves. If we can get beyond our conditioned reaction of using information to judge ourselves, then we can use everything in our experience to attempt to get a glimpse of *what it is that is perceiving*. We can use awareness to catch a glimpse of awareness.

Imagine this. Instead of using everything around you to gather information about what is wrong with you, what if everything reflected your interconnectedness with all life? Can you sense that the subject-object relationship would have shifted? Again, in the words of our Daily Recollection, that is "the joy of intelligence knowing itself"—a joy that is not available to us as long as we are looking at life in terms of what is wrong.

awakening

Sometimes I am asked about the differences between the Rinzai and Soto schools of Zen and between sudden and gradual enlightenment, with which they are associated. I belong to the Soto tradition, so naturally I support the gradual approach, and I cannot speak for Rinzai.

There is an idea that a sudden awakening experience, or enlightenment, can be so transformative that it alters personality, character, karma. I know of no evidence of that; an awakening experience does not necessarily change one's basic orientation to life. There does not seem to me to be a lot in what the Buddha taught to support making awakening the focus of one's practice. I suppose it is like reading the Bible: you can find something in there to make a case for or against almost anything, if you select your passages carefully enough. So, there may be stories about what the Buddha taught that would support a push toward awakening, but I do not know them.

In fact, I have never been able to understand how a concerted push toward enlightenment would serve anything other than ego-centricity. I have met people who claim to have had sudden awakening experiences, and it did not seem to have improved their lives in any way that made me want to adopt that approach. In fact, I have talked to people who have pretty much had their lives ruined over such things, because without a context, awakening can fall into categories like "amazing experiences" or "places I would like to live but don't." Having an extraordinary experience that nothing afterward ever measures up to can result in a lot of suffering.

I am in the trust-the-process club. I figure it all pretty much unfolds in the proper sequence and time framework as long as we are paying attention.

work

M any of us spend much of our day simply enduring what we do at work so we can get to some other experience that feels like our own. Because we put so much time and energy into something that feels external to us, it would be good to examine our belief systems about work. Where did they come from? Do we want to hold those beliefs? Do those beliefs match our experience?

There are two ways of being in the world that we consider in spiritual practice, and they are reflected in our attitudes toward work. One is the expansive, present, interconnected, blissful, relaxed, comfortable, peaceful way of being alive. The other is resisting. It involves an attitude like, "I've got to get it done. It doesn't matter if I like it. It has nothing really to do with me, and if I could get out of it I would." Within that attitude, we can be good sports, or we can feel resentful, or we can out-and-out hate it.

On retreat or in regular life, when we get a work assignment, our attitude can be the got-to-get-it-done way of approaching it, or it can be openness to doing something familiar in a different way. Work offers an opportunity to practice being in the body and with the breath and making the work a dance. We might ask ourselves, "Can I be joyful doing this? What is it about this task that isn't joyful? If I get the right job, is it automatically going to be joyful, and if I don't get that job, I can't feel joyful?"

Some people hold a belief that if you start enjoying your work assignment, you should try to look slightly depressed or someone will come along and notice and you will be moved to a job you hate. Then you would have to learn to be joyful in a whole new arena. Imagine that!

not minding minding

A retreatant described the suffering involved in turning compost. Gnats were in her eyes and ears and mouth and nose, she was standing in slime, and there was a terrible smell. She said, "I tried to imagine what it would be like not to mind all that."

We have to be careful not to idealize that kind of experience. It is perfectly natural to mind stench and slime and gnats in your nose. Not minding is a lot to expect. There is a part of you who hates gnats, and you can sympathize with her—but without suffering over it.

How about acknowledging that you do mind this experience, but not minding minding it?

outrageous information

I have been asked why we say "end suffering" rather than "end my suffering." There is a reason, but it is a tricky one. The suffering is not personal; it is universal. It is not possible to end one's own suffering and not end suffering. Now, that is one of those paradoxes that make me adore Zen.

There is a well-known saying by the thirteenth-century Zen master Dogen that goes something like this. "To study the dharma is to study the self. To study the self is to forget the self. To forget the self is to be enlightened by all things." Usually, that's all we hear, but the next line is, "To be enlightened by all things is to free one's body and mind and those of others."

If you work hard and end your suffering, yes, that ends my suffering, too, although it does not guarantee that I will know it. The illusion that creates a separate self is the same illusion that creates suffering. When we wake up, the illusion dies, and the suffering ends.

It is perfectly clear that not everyone has awakened. Imagine being in a dream with everyone else, and in that dream all sorts of horrible things are happening. You wake up, you see that everyone else is still dreaming, and you say to them, "Wake up! It's not real. It's just a bad dream." What you are likely to hear in response is, "Leave me alone, I'm sleeping."

"Even if we end our suffering," people will say, "won't other people all around the world still suffer horrible things?" Let's look at that from a different perspective. Think about a time pretty far back in the past when you really suffered over something. Let's say a relationship ended, which was very painful for you. Do you want that relationship now? Probably not. Are you upset that it is over? No. Imagine telling that younger you who is in the throes of a broken heart, "You'll be over this one day. It won't matter to you at all. You will go on and be happy and even grateful that that relationship is not part of your life, because you'll be freed up to have something else that you want more." Do you think for a second that the younger you would say, "Oh, thank you for clarifying that?"

In that example, we can see that we would not be able to stop the suffering of your younger self, even though from a larger perspective, that suffering is completely unnecessary. In the illusion of that time and place, the suffering exists. From another perspective, it does not exist. Both of those things are true. So, let us consider moving to a perspective from which it is possible to see that people suffer because people choose to suffer. That, I realize, is an outrageous statement, but suffering is the natural result of assuming identification with the illusion of a self that is separate.

In Buddhist sutras, we read about how a person comes up to the Buddha, bows deeply, drops to one knee, and says, "O Great Awakened One, please give me your teaching." The Buddha responds with a pithy saying that is uniquely appropriate to the time, place, and individual. Often it is something outrageous-sounding, like, "The seeing is in the seeing, the hearing is in the heard." Then the person does the decent thing and becomes enlightened on the spot and kisses the hem of the Buddha's robe in gratitude. It must have been very different twenty-five hundred years ago, because I can tell you that most of the people I know, when given similar pithy and appropriate and outrageous information, do not respond well at all.

How do we end suffering? By accepting everything, exactly as it is. Hearing that is like a knife in the heart. Inside we shriek, *no!* That is the shriek of the ego devoted to suffering. In fact, there is no choice other than accepting everything exactly as it is, because everything *is* exactly as it is. It is as simple as that. There is nowhere else to go.

But here is the good news: everybody who has taken that step of ending suffering reports that the result is bliss beyond description.

〰 8 the paradoxical heart 〰

Ogne of the fundamental paradoxes of Zen is that we discover compassion for others by finding compassion within ourselves, for ourselves. You can look all over the world, the Buddha said, and find no one more deserving of love than yourself. And in the moment of truly loving ourselves, there is nothing separate from or outside that love.

hard zen

Zen practice has a reputation for being hard, even harsh. And it has the right reputation, in this sense: it is indeed a harsh reality for egocentricity. For the personality, the illusion of a separate self that has managed with whatever degree of success to function in society, the entity that has been "born" and is going to "die" and sees every moment of life as a potential threat to its survival, Zen practice is a desolate, disturbing, terrifying experience. Zen practice is designed specifically to go after the core of egocentricity and dissolve it.

Now, there is also the soft, sweet, tender aspect of Zen, and that is the heart of the authentic self having its reaction to this practice. The heart knows that compassion is its true identity, that loving-kindness is its real expression, that it has not been born and it is not going to die, that it is eternal. Its only desire is to live in interconnectedness. Yet for most of us, for as long as we can remember, this heart of ours has been bound in service to the overpowering illusion of a separate self.

The Buddha talked about the miraculous nature of the realization that there is an alternative to suffering. Many people live their entire lives without a glimmer that there is another way than following what they have been conditioned to believe in attempting to survive. That they are trapped in a belief system that *may not be true* does not occur to them. To come into this life, to recognize that what one is experiencing is suffering, to realize that it is possible to end suffering, and to have the intelligence and aptitude and willingness and opportunity to pursue a path that leads away from suffering—that is the most extraordinary thing.

Some people come to Zen from having read about awakening and wanting to have that experience. Or Zen is the "in" thing to do; it is what the cool, sophisticated people do. But such motives are unlikely to sustain a person through serious spiritual practice.

Some people come to a path like this having sensed that they are not living well, that their "survival," in fact, is killing them. That can feel like despair in the heart. A lot of people talk to me about a deep longing they have always felt, a dissatisfaction with life as it is generally presented, a sense that there must be more than looking at the world and trying to decide which group of people killing which other group of people is right, which group we should support in killing which group. That cannot be what life is all about.

Some people are attracted to Zen *because* it sounds hard and harsh and demanding. One of my favorite stories was told by Jiyu-Kennett Roshi about a group of American men who went over to Japan for *sesshin,* an intensive meditation retreat. I picture them in whitewall haircuts, all revved up, gritting their teeth, ready for this grueling experience, determined to survive it, no matter how awful it is. When they arrive, they are invited to meet the Zen master. The master serves the men tea and sweet rolls, and he chats with them. But the Americans are all geared up to meditate, and they get restless with this tea party and small talk. The master serves more tea and chats some more. Finally, one poor guy can't stand it any longer, and he says, "This isn't what I came here for!" The master just looks at him, smiles, bows, and says softly, "Here, let me give you some more tea. And please have another sweet roll."

To me, Zen practice means going up against every way in which you are stuck in an identity as a separate self. If you want it to be hard, then what will be hard for you is that it is not very hard after all. We have a Catholic nun at our monastery who has had to confront her lifetime conviction that deprivation is equivalent to spirituality. In her Zen practice, she is required to buy things for herself. That makes her crazy, because it brings up conditioned responses that support the whole idea of a separate self. For people who are used to a long, hot shower every morning and time to iron out those last little wrinkles in their clothes, being on retreat or at the monastery and having limited time for a shower (and possibly limited hot water) and living in sweat clothes is part of their practice. Each of us brings to spiritual practice the issues we need to resolve. Those issues are simply who we are, what we have been doing and living. Whatever the issues are, they are confronted in spiritual practice.

When egocentricity does not get its way—which is what happens in a practice like this—it looks ahead and says, "Oh, no, am I going to be deprived of everything I want for the rest of my life?" We can recognize that that is the same force that has always made us miserable. And we can recognize spiritual practice as support for our hearts that has never been available before. Even though we struggle, even though we encounter rough patches along the path, at some level we know who's who and what's what.

In our hearts we know which side we are on and what we are trying to get through and what is available on the other side.

To the student who is confronting whatever it is in themselves that they need to work with, it can seem as if the teacher is engaged in some mysterious sort of torture. I tell people over and over, I do not stay awake at night plotting ways to torment them. People come to me saying, basically, "Here is my misery," then they are surprised when I can see it.

It is the teacher's job to pry each person loose from their conditioning. Whether the attachment is to greed or to deprivation, being required to move in the opposite direction—letting go of what they have, or allowing themselves to have—is a painful experience for ego. But that is the only way.

oneness

The idea that each of us has our own suffering could reinforce the idea of separateness, but it does not need to. We like to say, "This is me, this is mine, these are my boundaries." I am suggesting, though, that we take complete responsibility for everything.

In our precepts ceremony, we recite these lines (the Verse of Purification):

All harmful thoughts, words, and deeds,
since before the beginning of beginningless time,
having been born through body, mouth, and mind,
I openly acknowledge, accept, embrace, and let go.

That is, everything that has ever gone wrong, since before the beginning of beginningless time, is my responsibility. Not my fault, but my responsibility. I do not need to draw arbitrary lines around things and say, "Well, this much is my responsibility, but that part is yours. If you would stop doing that and if you were different, then we wouldn't have this problem." No: the whole thing is my responsibility. You do whatever you do.

What if we all took responsibility in that way? Then nothing would happen to you that did not happen to me, and nothing would happen to me that did not happen to you. Taking responsibility for all of it is an acknowledgement of oneness—the oneness that is our deepest experience and that we want never to lose sight of.

accept everything

Something I love about Zen is that a statement like "accept everything" does not *mean* anything.

People will ask, "Does 'accept everything' mean you should not try to change anything?" We want to take a statement that tells us something to do and apply it throughout our lives. But that statement has no application.

Accepting everything is like seeing without a particular object of sight; it is the seeing itself that is the point. Trying to *apply* the statement "accept everything" is like closing our eyes and wandering around in the dark again. Asking questions like, "Should I not try to change anything?" or "What should I do?" is the same movement into egocentricity, into separateness, away from what is.

There is no separation. There is only interconnection, with no inside and no outside. "Where do I stand to get a look at that?" we want to know. There again is the movement back into egocentricity, into separateness. We are always trying to position ourselves so that we can have a view of something that cannot be seen by someone who is separate from it.

heaven and hell

We have the ability to plunge ourselves into hell by something as simple as not liking how something looks or sounds. Actually, what we do not like is our attitude about it, and we would prefer to hold on to our attitudes than to be in heaven. For the ego, it is more important to be right than happy.

There may have been a time in your life when an awful thing happened, and you find yourself going back to it and reliving the pain and fear and humiliation. No matter how good a person you try to be, when you make that descent, it is hellish. We may attempt to remind ourselves that heaven also exists, but ego does not want to hear that, resists the whole idea, thinks it is stupid—all those things ego does to continue in its own world of separation. When we are out of the present moment, lost in ego, we *are* non-acceptance, we *are* shaming, we are all those conditioned identities that constitute hell.

The secret is, don't go there. Hell is not going to change. Our only hope is in staying away from it.

Here is an old Zen story. The samurai comes to the Zen master. He wants to know about heaven and hell. The Zen master says, "Why should I teach a bozo like you?" The samurai is enraged. He reaches for his sword, ready to kill the Zen master. The Zen master bows and says, "There open the gates of hell." The samurai thinks for a second, and a big smile comes over his face. The Zen master then bows and says, "And there open the gates of heaven."

So, it does not take much to go right from heaven to hell. The raising of an eyebrow and you are in heaven; the raising of an eyebrow and you are in hell.

For me, it is comforting to be aware that the trip from hell to heaven is just as quick as the trip in the opposite direction. It is as simple—it really is—as recognizing those two places.

present in catastrophe

Somebody described to me being in a hurricane and noticing that she was fully present to the experience and even enjoying it. Afterwards, though, she was depressed, and she had a long list of things that had to be done.

How could it be that someone feels free and lets go and enjoys life during a catastrophe? Well, it is hard to take a hurricane personally. In a catastrophe, there is no "you," because there is nothing to be in relationship to. There is nothing you can do about it; there is nothing for you to be. Things are completely out of control, so you might as well accept it and let it all be as it is. Once you do that, it is perfectly blissful. Afterward, making the long list of things to be done is a reaction against that bliss, and then when ego reasserts control, it is depressing.

People talk about this same kind of experience in war or in being with someone who is dying. When everything else falls away, there is only whatever is there in the moment. In fact, even though the content might be defined as negative, people will refer to those as peak experiences in their lives. For that little period of time, there was no room for separateness.

I read something like this: "Rest is receiving all of life without judgment." That is what one is forced to do in a hurricane—just rest. There is no place for judgment, and without judgment there is no resistance; there is nothing separate. There is just oneness.

what will sustain us?

I never try to talk anybody into doing spiritual practice, because you need to know it is something you do for yourself. As long as you believe that you can be sustained by lying on the couch with a book and a cup of coffee or calling somebody and going somewhere to eat, you will believe doing those things is a way of taking care of yourself. Attempts to meditate will come from the childish belief that you should do it because that is what a good person does.

When life gets rough enough, however, and you turn to your book and your cup of coffee and your phone calls and find they do not sustain you, then you realize that you have nothing to turn to. As in any relationship, if you have not put time and energy and effort into your spiritual practice, you cannot expect it to support you when you need it. You must work on that relationship when you do not need it.

Eventually you know from your own experience what will sustain you, what you can turn to under any circumstances, what will not fail you no matter how tired or sick or confused or depressed you become. What will sustain you is your spiritual practice.

I have learned so much from being with people in the process of dying. Sylvia, one of the members of our sangha, said that she had had a rather romantic image of death: she imagined that she would lie in her bed and look out her window and read books she loved and listen to music she loved and slowly pass out of this reality and into the next. It never occurred to her that she would be able to read and not want to. It never occurred to her that she would not be able to bear the sound of music. It never occurred to her that the things that were the greatest comfort in life would bring no comfort in dying.

I also remember being with my cousin as he died. He was such a social fellow, and it fell upon me to turn people away who wanted to see him. He could not bear to tell people that to be with them was too tiring for him.

For me, those incidents reaffirm my commitment to a practice that I know will be there for me even when I no longer have an interest in all the other things I cared about. No matter what the circumstances, I can always find that place of refuge inside and go there and have that sense of well-being.

freeing the heart

In spiritual practice we have to be willing to be a little bit foolish, to take risks, to be embarrassed, to be emotional. It is like falling in love. When you fall in love, you are willing to be foolish, and you really do not care, because you have nothing to lose. The emotions are flying every which way, out of control, but you are really alive. If we have to maintain control, then we can know that we are maintaining egocentricity, because only egocentricity has an interest in control.

Egocentricity presents the view that it is saving us, protecting us, making sure that we get what we want and have the right kind of life. What is really going on is the heart wanting to be open but being encased in and constricted by the armor of egocentricity. Spiritual practice attempts to reach our hearts, but it has trouble getting through egocentricity, which says things like, "What kind of life would that be, going into the monastery? You would have to give up everything. Who knows what could happen to you? That's not something you want to do." It is difficult to realize that that is not the voice of your heart. That voice is what stands between you and your heart.

It is good to remind ourselves of that: *egocentricity is what stands between me and my heart.*

pleasure for joy

Someone asked me if we had any fun activities at the monastery like volleyball or singing or foot massage. The answer is no. We live almost entirely in silence and largely in solitude. The only times we speak are in personal guidance and in group discussions, and in functional communication with the work director.

The reason is not that there is anything wrong with fun activities, but that in monastic training we are attempting something very unusual. Instead of participating in an activity that brings pleasure, that makes us feel connected, that creates joy, we are learning to live in such a way that all activity brings pleasure, all activity makes us feel connected, all activity creates joy. We practice awareness of what we do, in whatever activity, that prevents us from experiencing the joy and interconnectedness that we might seek in dancing or singing or interacting with people.

When a person is as happy as a person can be doing anything at all at any moment of the day or night, it is because that interconnectedness is constantly sensed. The person is not feeling separate and needing some activity to produce a temporary sense of connection. Many activities that are supposed to bring a feeling of connectedness in fact leave us feeling separate, isolated, lonely. But if that interconnectedness is the focus of one's moment-by-moment experience, then there is nothing that does not fit into that.

silent together

Being in silence together brings consciousness to areas of life that we never have the opportunity to experience in the regular world. For example, we tend to believe that if we were getting nonstop compliments, we would be happy, and if we were giving nonstop compliments, people around us would be happy.

On a silent retreat, it is wonderful to be around people who are experiencing a lot of inward joy. They are not saying anything, and there is nothing particular in their body language, but you can just feel it. You like to stand near them or walk by them or just sense their presence on the next cushion.

We come on silent retreat and learn that it is not necessary to be constantly getting or giving compliments or affirming one another's existence. There is another way of being with people that is so deeply meaningful that almost everybody who experiences it wants more of it.

form and emptiness

The climactic line of the Heart Sutra, which is chanted every day in many Zen monasteries, is, "Form is emptiness, emptiness is not different from form." What does that mean?

Somebody asked me that question, and I asked him what he thought it meant. He said, "Sometimes a feeling or an attitude that seems very solid arises out of nothingness. Nothing was there, and then something was there. There is also the opposite experience of being in the midst of something that seems to have great solidity, like fear, and it falling away into nothingness." But he thought there must be more to it than that. If there is not more to it than that, why would people have been reciting that line for twenty-five hundred years?

But what if there is not any more to it than that?

The implications are enormous. It would mean that in every moment I am caught up in the content of an issue, feeling, "This is real, this is me, this is mine," behind that, through that, in the middle of that, is spaciousness. Pure spaciousness.

Picture this. Everything, starting right here at the edge of what I call "me" and going forever, is just what it is, as it is. Then something comes along, and I focus my consciousness on it. Boom— it is "real." With the focusing of my consciousness, that thing comes into existence. Then my consciousness leaves it, and it simply dissolves back into that stuff-soup of all that is.

What that thing was before my consciousness touched it, we cannot say, because if we say it, consciousness has touched it. We could call it "emptiness," in the sense that it is empty of any quality or characteristic, empty of any particular or separate identity, until I make it "form." So here we are, our consciousness lighting on thing after thing after thing, each thing being no-thing until it is brought into some-thing by consciousness.

Just as fascinating as consciousness bringing form from emptiness is that I am the center of the universe, creating time and space with my consciousness. In a wonderful little book called *On Having No Head,* the author describes walking along and suddenly realizing that he has no head. That is outrageously significant in that it speaks to the belief system we operate in and how we choose our beliefs over reality. You "know" you have a head because you have seen it in a mirror, and you "know" it because you can see that everyone else has one. But from your own direct experience, you cannot know it. You can look down and see this stalk-like body, but you can see it only up to chest level, and then—there is the universe. The body is like a platform with the sensory apparatus mounted on it. It opens out on top to every-thing you can know, as far as you can see, as far as you can hear, as far as you can imagine. All that—everything—is sitting right on top of this body-stalk.

Now, here is the fun part. The body-stalk is *part of* that universe that is experienced as resting on the top of it; it is contained within that expansive reality that is all you actually know. Here we have a wonderful example of "form is emptiness; emptiness is not different from form." All form exists within that spacious expanse;

there is one container seemingly without limits and another seemingly limited, within that limitlessness, yet the limitlessness is not available without the limited. Without the ability to create time and space in that way (the illusion of time and space, actually), there is no "this body," and without the body, there is no universe. In the words of Meister Eckhart, once again, "The eyes with which I see God, God sees me."

We waste a lot of time focused on that which makes the limitless seem to disappear and makes the limited—namely, me—the only thing that exists. We turn away from the limitless by just having a thought about what is coming up today that we do not like, or who said what, or anything that is not the way we want it to be. In an instant, all of that expansiveness, that oneness, that joy is gone.

In this practice, we learn that in the next instant we can return to that reality, that no matter what we are doing we can experience the interplay of that mystery.

karma

Karma is usually understood to mean cause and effect. I do this, that is the result.

I feel quite confident that that is so—that there is, on one level, cause and effect. The difficulty is that life does not happen on only one level, and few of us can see the entire picture.

It seems to me that karma is a concept we have adopted because it is simply too anxiety-producing to admit that we are powerless and without control. Karma is like a grid we mentally place over life to give us the illusion that we have an understanding of what is going on. We use the idea of karma in an attempt to comprehend the incomprehensible.

Cause and effect is the experience of an entity that believes itself to be separate. The self sees its experience as the reference point and all of life in relationship to that reference point. Therefore one thing happens after another *as that self perceives it.* Does that in fact happen? Yes, within the illusion of that "separate" self, it does happen.

We are the sum total of everything it has taken to produce us from before the beginning of beginningless time. Our conditioning teaches us to experience life in a linear, sequential manner, one thing following the other. But life also happens in dimensions that are not linear. The sum total of everything it has taken to produce us leaves nothing out—including the illusion of a separate self. Everything is encompassed in that interconnectedness.

We are all familiar with the question, "If a tree fell in the forest and there were no one there to hear it, would there be a sound?" Here is my offering: If there were no illusion of a self who is separate from all that is, would there be cause and effect? Would there be karma? And—buckle your seat belt—would there be right and wrong?

In the final analysis, karma is simply a notion encouraging us to look in a particular direction. Karma is what we call what is. Karma is the way we try to sort out life into manageable relationships. There is no problem with that, as long as we remember that we are making it all up, as long as we do not believe any of it.

no answer, no formula, no magic wand

Our lives are lived in such a mind-boggling struggle against what is obvious: what is, is, and there is nothing to be done about it. Without the dualistic notion of someone who is separate to have an opinion about it, would what is still be what is? We cannot be sure, but we guess the answer is, yes.

The whole struggle exists because we think we should be other than the way we are, we think our lives should be different from what they are. All suffering arises from that illusion. As far as I can tell, there is no proof that anything should or could be different from the way it is.

In my less clear moments, I wish I had a magic wand with which I could take away all suffering. But it is a comfort for me to know that things are not going to be any different from what they are. We cannot hold on to anything; it all slips away. In a moment of being centered, we recognize that ease and well-being and sufficiency. Then we slip back into our conditioning.

For me, to have an expectation of something else makes it worse. To think that I am going to learn something or I will have something that I can apply, that my life will be different if I can just remember some formula—that is simply not how it is.

So, lower your expectations. And be kinder to yourself than you think you should be.

letting go into cheerfulness

P eople are prisoners of "I can't." One of the best things about monastic training is that you do not get to say "I can't." It does not matter a flying fig how you feel. If you are tired, you may have less fun than if you are full of energy, but you are going to show up anyway and do what needs to be done.

At ten o'clock at night, when you are tired and the garbage has to be taken out, you can do it cheerfully or uncheerfully. The choice is yours. It is amazing how quickly you can learn to do it cheerfully.

We hope that by staying stuck in our conditioning we will have a different choice—like, it is ten o'clock, we are tired, the garbage needs to be taken out, and by feeling really miserable we somehow will not have to do it. But regardless of how we feel, sooner or later, the garbage has to go out.

In regular life, we may whine and wheedle and beg, and eventually someone else will take the garbage out. But that is not uplifting behavior. In the monastery, there is nobody else we can manipulate into doing what we do not want to do. It is up to us, so we simply get off it.

That is a wonderfully liberating experience. We hear the voice start in with how tired we are, and we just respond, "So?"

The voice gets insistent: "Maybe I could just leave it here until tomorrow. . ."

"Ah."

"But I cannot do one more thing tonight!"

"Hm."

When we go right ahead and take the garbage out anyway, we find that there is an endless supply of willingness.

the same

People say that monastic life must be terribly hard because it is the same thing day after day. It is true that the schedule is the same every day, but how unconscious would you have to be to think one day is like another one? However, it is the case that it is up to you to bring the enjoyment to it. The schedule itself is not going to entertain you.

Sameness is an interesting subject to explore. Let's say you have a videotape of one movie, and you watch it over and over. At what point would you start feeling you couldn't stand it—the tenth time you saw it? The twentieth? But what if you watched it in a whole different way? You might begin by following what happens in just the top left corner, then you could watch it again and keep your attention on the top right corner. You could just listen to the music. You could watch for the red colors in every scene. You could focus on eyebrows or horizons or particular words or tones of voice. You could be fascinated for a lifetime with a single movie if you were really present to it.

That is what we can get out of the sameness of something like a daily schedule. Of course, egocentricity goes crazy with sameness—and that is precisely the point.

People ask how I can say the same things over and over without running out of patience. That is always a surprise to me. I do not know I am saying the same things over and over. I think they are new and interesting every single time. I am as fascinated with them as I could possibly be, because they arise out of the moment I am in, and so they are breathtakingly appropriate. I am constantly in awe of the fact that such clarity is available in every moment.

Each of those moments in which we are truly present makes us want more of those moments. Pretty soon, we realize that when things are too different all the time, we are distracted, and it is hard to maintain our focus, hard to stay present.

Once we no longer want to be distracted, once we want our atmosphere to be as conducive to being present as we can possibly make it, how can we have that? By keeping the same schedule, by minimizing the variables—that is what increases the chances of our being present.

Then, as we are increasingly present, we realize that there is nothing the same about it. Every carrot we chop in the kitchen is a new miracle when we give it our full attention. It is only when we are not present to it that we feel, "Oh, no, another carrot."

seeing goodness

A n important part of spiritual practice is understanding the inherent goodness of this person that you are watching, yourself.

It is difficult not to take ourselves personally, because the part of us who looks at ourselves does so from a perspective of judgment, assuming that at our core is *not* inherent goodness. We conclude that something about us is faulty, something is flawed, something needs to be fixed.

Here is an exercise to remind yourself that your inherent nature, your essence, is goodness: project goodness outward. Look around at the other people you know and be aware of their goodness. It may be easier in a group of strangers on retreat than with the people we see every day, because we know the little foibles and flaws of those close to us. With them, we tend to make the same argument that we make about ourselves: "I'm not sure that inherent goodness really is the bottom line in this case. This person may actually need modification."

At a retreat, though, when we look around at the people who have gathered, all we need to know is that out of all the things they could have done for two or five or ten days, they chose to spend it in meditation. Knowing that, how could we look at them and assume that they are motivated by anything other than goodness?

If we look at somebody and assume inherent evil and then try to figure out what is motivating that person based on that assumption, we are going to reach some pretty alarming conclusions. But with goodness as a basic assumption, when we ask what might be motivating a person, all kinds of possibilities open up. When we wonder why that person is doing whatever they are doing, we see it in a kinder light. Maybe they are worried, maybe their feelings have been hurt, maybe life is hard for them, maybe they do not feel understood. We can guess that the reason somebody is being irritating in a particular moment is that they are struggling with something, they are suffering over something. We do not have to know the particulars of it to know that we do not need to be mean to them. We do not need to be another point of suffering in their life. They are already suffering; that is why they are being difficult.

The result of this exercise in projecting goodness is to settle for a rather broad conclusion: there is never any reason for blame. We are all doing the best we can.

It is a whole new world of goodness, outside you and inside you. And of course those are the same.